MESSAGING
MATTERS

How School Leaders Can Inspire Teachers,
Motivate Students, and Reach Communities

WILLIAM D. PARKER

Solution Tree | Press

a division of

Solution Tree

555 North Morton Street
Bloomington, IN 47404
800.733.6786 (toll free) / 812.336.7700
FAX: 812.336.7790

email: info@SolutionTree.com
SolutionTree.com

Visit **go.SolutionTree.com/leadership** to download the free reproducibles in this book.

Printed in the United States of America

21   20   19   18   2   3   4   5

Library of Congress Cataloging-in-Publication Data

Names: Parker, William D., 1969- author.
Title: Messaging matters : how school leaders can inspire teachers, motivate students, and reach communities / William D. Parker.
Description: Bloomington, IN : Solution Tree Press, [2017] | Includes bibliographical references and index.
Identifiers: LCCN 2017013959 | ISBN 9781945349096 (perfect bound)
Subjects: LCSH: Educational leadership. | Communication in education. | School management and organization. | School administrators--Professional relationships.
Classification: LCC LB2806 .P356 2017 | DDC 371.2--dc23 LC record available at https://lccn.loc.gov/2017013959

Solution Tree
Jeffrey C. Jones, CEO
Edmund M. Ackerman, President

Solution Tree Press
President and Publisher: Douglas M. Rife
Editorial Director: Sarah Payne-Mills
Managing Production Editor: Caroline Cascio
Senior Production Editor: Suzanne Kraszewski
Senior Editor: Amy Rubenstein
Copy Editor: Miranda Addonizio
Proofreader: Evie Madsen
Text and Cover Designer: Laura Cox
Editorial Assistants: Jessi Finn and Kendra Slayton

ACKNOWLEDGMENTS

My first conversation about this book happened in 2016 when Claudia Wheatley from Solution Tree Press reached out to me by phone. Always on the lookout for new authors, Claudia told me that I had developed a "large digital footprint" with the online content I was sharing with school leaders via my blog and podcast. As we talked about my school culture and how communication strategies had helped shaped its momentum, she suggested the title for a new book on the subject: *Messaging Matters*.

The title struck a chord with me. Four years earlier, I had made a commitment that I wanted to connect with others and grow personally and professionally by sharing at least one blog post every week for five years on lessons I was learning in school leadership. That decision enhanced my communication about my school and about school leadership in ways I had never imagined. The more I highlighted the great lessons and actions of my teachers, students, and team members, the more momentum was built around positive initiatives.

At this point, the bulk of my writing experience had been in the world of blogging, podcasting, and self-publishing so I was thrilled at the idea of a book with Solution Tree Press. I also had no idea how challenging and encouraging it would be to be surrounded by so many eyes, minds, thoughts, suggestions, and corrections along the way. *Messaging Matters* has definitely been a team effort: it could not have happened without the students, teachers, and other education leaders who inspire me every day. It could not have happened without the many reviewers who provided incredible feedback. I have so many people to thank for this project.

Thank you, Reverend Blake Altman and Trinity Presbyterian, for giving me free use of office space on the weekends and holidays to finish this book. Thank you, Richard and Carol Spears, for the use of your farmhouse where I drafted many parts of this book during holidays with my family.

Thank you, Claudia Wheatley, for inspiring the idea for this book and consistently giving warm and patient guidance. Also, sincere thanks to Douglas Rife for generously taking a risk on this practicing principal who believed he could write a book while still leading a school. Thank you, Amy Rubenstein, for offering amazing editorial wisdom, and Sue Kraszewski for providing brilliant editorial and production direction. And to the entire Solution Tree Press team: thank you for enveloping me into a family of professionals who love promoting the best in educational ideas, innovation, and inspiration!

Of course, a project like this also meant sacrificing a lot of time with my family and school. You have no idea, really. So thank you, Skiatook Public Schools administration, teachers, staff, students, and parents, for entrusting me with the privilege of serving and for allowing me to share in the joys of watching students learn and grow.

And thank you to my amazing wife, Missy, whom I can never repay for supporting me while writing this book. Thank you for being by my side during my crazy life as an educator for the past twenty-four years. You are my best friend. And to our four children: Emily, Mattie, Katie, and Jack. Thank you for loving me. May you grow up to live for God's glory and to love life so much that you can't help but celebrate every day!

Robbie Hooker
Executive Director for High
  School Leadership
Henry County Schools
McDonough, Georgia

Laura Jennaro
Principal
Milton Middle School
Milton, Wisconsin

Kim Spychalla
Principal
MacArthur Elementary School
Green Bay, Wisconsin

Visit **go.SolutionTree.com/leadership** to download the free reproducibles in this book.

TABLE OF CONTENTS

ABOUT THE AUTHOR

 **William D. Parker** is executive director of the Oklahoma Association of Secondary School Principals and Oklahoma Middle Level Educators Association. He is former principal of Skiatook High School, just north of Tulsa, Oklahoma. As a high school teacher, he taught language arts, creative writing, and advanced placement English. He has also taught writing in summer student academies through Oklahoma State University's College of Osteopathic Medicine, and he has taught adult education courses through the Tulsa Technology Center.

An Oklahoma educator since 1993, he was named Broken Arrow Public School's South Intermediate High School Teacher of the Year in 1998. He became an assistant principal in 2004. A member of the National Association of Secondary School Principals, Will was named the 2011 Oklahoma Assistant Principal of the Year. As principal of a Title I school, his school's innovative approaches to collaboration, remediation, and mentoring have resulted in marked improvements in student performance. He is regularly asked to speak to principal associations, school leadership conferences, and graduate classes on effective leadership practices, organizational behavior, and digital tools for enhancing school communication.

Will hosts a weekly podcast called *Principal Matters* and writes a weekly blog that he shares on www.williamdparker.com, his website. He is also a contributing author on *Connected Principals* (http://connected principals.com) and a guest blogger for the National Association of Secondary School Principals. He hosts monthly webinars free (www .ccosa.org/index.php?brunch-learn-leadership-webinars) for the members of the Cooperative Council for Oklahoma School Administration, his state's principal association, so they can connect and share innovative ideas for growing in school leadership.

Will earned his bachelor's degree in English education from Oral Roberts University in Tulsa, Oklahoma, and his master's degree in education leadership from Northeastern State University in Tahlequah, Oklahoma.

To book William D. Parker for professional development, contact pd@SolutionTree.com.

INTRODUCTION

Why Messaging Matters

The art of communication is the language of leadership.

—James Humes

In a January 29, 2015, episode of *Invisibilia*, a National Public Radio podcast about the invisible forces that affect us without our awareness, reporters spoke about a phenomenon known as *entanglement*. The conversation began with a description of a physics experiment in which scientists were able to isolate atoms in separate locations, change the molecular structure, and manipulate the two separate atoms into becoming one atom, though still in separate locations (Miller & Spiegel, 2015).

That's right: atoms contained in boxes four feet away from one another demonstrated simultaneous responses. These atoms are not mirror images of one another, however; they *are* one another—separate but one. This is entanglement. Charles Q. Choi (2015), in a *Live Science* article titled "Quantum Record! 3,000 Atoms Entangled in Bizarre State," explains that scientists theorize entangled atoms may stay connected even if they are a universe apart.

Scientists are able to explain *how* to make this happen, but they still cannot explain *why* this is possible. So, why should you be fascinated with this idea of entanglement? Well, before I answer that question, let me describe another entanglement phenomenon. This may seem like common sense, but *Invisibilia* reporters also explain how psychologists have proven that a person's environment influences his or her unconscious behavior—a kind of social entanglement (Miller & Spiegel, 2015).

In one example from the podcast, an unsuspecting individual enters an elevator with groups of people who exhibit predetermined movements (like facing the wrong direction or taking their hats off at the same time). Over and over again, and with multiple test cases, the individuals follow the movements of the group. Interestingly, they are not just responding to the group's movements (unconsciously taking the same actions as the group), but they are also simultaneously following their actions.

For instance, an individual wearing a hat enters an elevator with a group of people wearing hats. Without any advance notice, the hatted folks reach up and remove their hats, and the unsuspecting individual follows suit—often without any hesitation and often at the very same time! What is the explanation for this phenomenon? Entanglement.

So why is entanglement important to educators or school leaders interested in messaging? In a world of easy access to information, the way we communicate is critically important. Our words—conversations, announcements, praise, criticism, celebration, and so on—frame the message others hear about you and your school. *Messaging* is the mindset that defines the way you communicate. It is the platform you use for promoting what others perceive and believe about you or your school. This messaging is entangled in everything you do and say. In some ways, experiments with entanglement confirm what we've always known: our surroundings influence us more than we often recognize. We may connect with one another in ways more mysterious than we've ever imagined. In other ways, entanglement opens our eyes to incredible possibilities in how we communicate and influence others (Parker, 2015a).

Here's a simple application. If you take the idea of entanglement to its logical conclusion, you must seriously grapple with the power of your position as a school leader and ask yourself some questions.

- "What persons or ideas consistently surround me, and how do these affect who I am?"
- "How do I purposely and intentionally influence my home, work, and surroundings to bring about the most positive outcomes possible?"
- "How do I tailor messages within the school environment—to teachers, students, and the community—to reflect the true culture of the school?"

As school leaders, we cannot ignore how incredibly (and sometimes mysteriously) significant a part we each play in molding the school environment. We can accomplish this molding in many ways, but I can't think of a more powerful way than messaging. The messages teachers, staff members, students, parents, and the community receive about your school culture shape their perception of the school, your leadership, and often their general opinion about education and schooling. As a school leader, it is your responsibility to positively influence the messages the school community consistently receives. You are part of a web of entangled messages and influences; how can you meaningfully play your part?

Entanglement has many implications. In the *Invisibilia* episode, scientists ask if it is possible for bits of ourselves to actually be present in the places or people with whom we are entangled—like the same atom present in two separate locations (Miller & Spiegel, 2015). Regardless of how strange or mind blowing those implications may be, one of the most powerful takeaways is simply that the people and places all around us are consciously and unconsciously entangled.

Ask yourself if you are intentional about the messaging you send about your school—both within the walls and to the community beyond them. What part do your messages play in building and supporting a positive school culture?

A Messaging Crisis

Many schools are facing a leadership crisis—not because there are no strong leaders in schools but because school leaders often do not connect with the most powerful learning moments happening in their schools, nor celebrate them. Most school leaders feel overwhelmed, overworked, and overcommitted. With the ever-increasing responsibilities of the school principal, it should be no surprise that in 2012, the Center for Public Education found that the average principal stays on the job for five years or fewer (Hull, 2012).

A school leader's job often involves putting out situational fires, responding to urgent needs, or satisfying the requests of a multitude of stakeholders. It's no wonder that school leaders must battle for time to enjoy the best parts of school—being with the students and teachers who experience amazing moments of learning and celebrating them.

Even as school leaders learn to prioritize time for the most meaningful moments of school, difficult or negative situations often make it into conversations, social media, or mainstream media. As a result, the public gains a mistaken perception that schools are generally failing.

In Richard DuFour's (2015) book *In Praise of American Educators*, he explores this popular but misguided notion that schools are failing and cites a Gallup poll asking parents how they would grade American schools:

> The majority of parents gave Ds or Fs to U.S. schools. But when these same parents were asked how they would grade their own local school, the overwhelming majority assigned As or Bs . . . slightly more than 1 percent have indicated the [local] school is failing. (DuFour, 2015, p. 18)

Why is there such disparity between the perceptions of schools at large and particular local schools? Part of the reason rests with how the media generally portrays schools negatively. Also the current political divide in the United States has created incentives for politicians or lobbyists to emphasize negatives that work to their political advantage. Regardless of the reason, these larger perceptions drive public opinion. Public opinion drives public policy. And public policy provides or doesn't provide resources for our schools. Schools are providing amazing service to students, but that message is not always making it beyond the school or local community. What would happen if a movement began among school leaders to make messaging a higher priority? Imagine a different scenario for the larger perception of America's schools.

- What would happen if school leaders prioritized the incredible learning opportunities, the meaningful human connections, and the powerful engagement of their schools while strategically promoting, publishing, and celebrating those moments?

- What would happen if school leaders across a community, state, nation, or the globe committed to the same goal of encouraging and sharing positive moments?

- What would happen if you influenced the perceptions of your school or district based on overwhelming positive outcomes rather than negative, isolated incidents?

- What would happen if you were able to brand your school or district, promote your successes, and build the public's perception based on the good outcomes instead of the negative ones?

If you will ever be able to prioritize these positive moments and shift the direction of public policy in support of schools, you might start a national or global movement. But to do so, you must address two leadership issues.

1. You must prioritize and strategize time for doing what matters.

2. You must believe that messaging matters by understanding a comprehensive approach to building healthy school cultures and overwhelming others with the positive performances and celebrations of your students.

A New Era of Messaging

I wrote this book with the school principal in mind when I was a school principal. But the ideas in these pages can help all school leaders: superintendents, directors, instructional coaches, and teacher leaders. If you are reading this book because you simply want ideas for innovative communication tools, you may get more than you bargained for. My definition of messaging is much more extensive. This book is a comprehensive approach to building healthy schools that requires digging deeply into the motivations of your leadership, the value of listening to others, and the power of seeing your school through the eyes of others. It also involves building a collaborative community in which you consistently cultivate an environment of mutual respect, goal setting, and celebration. At the same time, this book is practical. I will share plenty of ideas on actions and tools you can begin to use immediately to improve your messaging.

After more than two decades as an educator and more than half those years in school administration, I've witnessed the positive and negative perceptions that school leaders can create among students, teachers, parents, community members, and colleagues. As a principal, blogger, author, podcaster, and speaker, I've also seen the powerful connections, growth, and energy of other leaders who have learned to maximize their communication platforms.

My own story is just one of many. I have taught in large and small schools. I began my career as a high school English teacher. I eventually began working on a master's degree in school administration and became a high school assistant principal in a school with fourteen hundred students. During the writing and publication of this book, I was principal of Skiatook High School in a city north of Tulsa, Oklahoma. (As this book went to press, I transitioned to the position of executive director of the Oklahoma Association of Secondary School Principals and Oklahoma Middle Level Educators Association.) With 750 students in grades 9–12 at Skiatook, messaging became an important part of my leadership. Each year we strategized with student leaders and teachers on mottos, announcements, and celebrations. We provided constant feedback on the wins we saw every day in student learning and activities. We worked hard to create a culture of collaboration, engagement, and positive entanglement. Skiatook has more than eight hundred parents who subscribe to weekly newsletters. It uses a variety of social media channels to promote a culture of learning and excellence. As a result, I like to describe the school community as *raving fans* of the school.

Over the years, I have spoken and presented to many groups of aspiring principals, school leaders, and student leaders. I also reach out to thousands of others around the globe through blogging, writing, podcasting, and posting on social media. Of all the interactions I have with others, the most common are those with my school community members and colleagues about the learning, activities, and celebrations happening in our school—not the drama, discipline, or difficulties. I believe this powerful form of messaging can benefit every school. That collaboration, relationship building, and celebration can be the norm for any school leader committed to the power of sending a message about school culture.

An Opportunity for Positive Entanglement

Today we have incredible capacity for building positive entanglements with members of our school community and celebrating our schools. Using social media, blogging, publishing, networking, and marketing are no longer tools or skills limited to corporate or business interests. Schools have amazing opportunities to leverage all these tools as well. But the journey begins by investing in your teachers, students, parents, and community through meaningful connections. That makes the message you have to deliver authentic and worth celebrating.

Perhaps you've already caught the wave of messaging power for your school. Or perhaps you are reading this book because you are interested in why messaging matters. Or maybe you want more strategies for improving your own communication influence. In the chapters that follow, you will find more than just tips on using digital tools. You will find strategies for effective communication, but more important, you'll discover why messaging matters. When you make a commitment as chief communicator to your students, teachers, team members, and community, amazing things begin to happen.

- Negative interactions can become the exception instead of the rule.

- Students and team members engage more in what matters most.

- Schools celebrate powerful learning opportunities instead of hiding them.

In addition, strong messaging allows your leadership influence to grow in the following ways. You will:

- Communicate expectations in advance and increase your ability to navigate your entire school year before it begins

- Deal with challenges in a positive way

- Provide meaningful feedback to teachers

- Enhance your school's image with digital tools

- Promote effective strategies that work

- Improve student behavior and performance

If you're going to maintain a positive perspective on school leadership that keeps you committed for the long term, you need motivation and strategies for improving the platform for your message. How can you make that happen? First, you create a positive culture through your entanglements. Second, you celebrate that positivity one message at a time.

How This Book Is Organized

I have divided this book into three parts to help you learn to maximize your messaging: (1) with teachers, (2) with students, and (3) with parents and the world. Each part contains a Now It's Your Turn section that contains questions for reflection and taking action. You will also see suggestions for digital tools throughout with ideas for ways to create effective online platforms.

If you read no further than this introduction, let me leave you with this question: What kind of lasting impression do you want to impart to your students, teachers, parents, and the community from and about your school? My fear is that many principals become so distracted in the tasks of school management that they lose sight of the importance of taking back the conversations about their schools. What about you? If you are ready to take new steps toward building powerfully positive entanglements and persuasive messages in your leadership, then read ahead and let's learn together how your messaging matters.

Now It's Your Turn

- In what ways do you intentionally work to keep your environment positive?

- In what ways have you already embedded practices into your school for cultivating strong relationships and promoting positive happenings?

- What is one step you can take today toward improving the entanglement experiences of students and teachers in your building?

Building a Positive Culture for Messaging

The less people know, the more they yell.

—Seth Godin

When I was a boy, I loved lying on the front porch at night. With no streetlights or neighbors, our West Tennessee farmhouse was enveloped in darkness, surrounded by swampy creeks and woods, accompanied by the sound of crickets and the serenade of spring frogs. The blanket of stars above me was a thick, mesmerizing maze of constellations. My dad went through a phase of interest in telescopes, so sometimes we took turns looking for planets or peering at the moon.

Did you know that only one side of the moon is visible from the Earth? Because of the Earth's orbit and the moon's speed of rotation while orbiting, we never see the other side of the moon. Just like we only see one side of the moon, all of us operate in contexts that no one else is able to see. This is especially true of leaders.

So, as leaders, how do we communicate as effectively and thoroughly as we can while accepting that sometimes misunderstandings still exist? How do we set a foundation for effective communication in our schools?

Cultivate the Characteristics of Great Leaders

In the classic business bestseller *Good to Great: Why Some Companies Make the Leap . . . and Others Don't*, Jim Collins (2001) examines the highest-performing companies at the turn of the 20th century to see what traits they have in common. You might be thinking, "Schools are not businesses"; however, educators can learn a lot from Collins's findings. As you focus on being the chief messenger in your school or district, consider the following lessons from Collins (2001).

Understand Your Passion and Mission, Which Drives Your Service Goals

According to Collins's (2001) research on the top companies in America, when an organization narrows its focus to one or two main areas, performance inevitably increases. Schools and companies have similar challenges. School leaders have a lot to accomplish, and in the mix of opportunities, leaders can sometimes lose focus on the main reason the school exists. This is why successful companies have leaders whose passion and mission are intertwined. When you focus your energy, talents, and creativity toward the most important outcomes in your school (student learning, for instance), then you have a mission that keeps you focused on what needs to be consistently communicated to others about your school. Your passion must be connected to your mission, or you are simply managing, not leading. Think about the main mission of your school. How do you keep the mission in focus in every decision and action you make for your school community? Do you express your mission in every communication you send to your staff, students, and community? If leaders can keep the main thing *the main thing* within their schools, then everyone has a better chance of reaching desired outcomes. One way I have included mission in my messaging with parents is with a section in my newsletter called Learning & Growing that features photos and updates on lessons teachers and students are completing throughout the school. Because student learning is the main thing, what you are passionate about communicating must include moments of such learning.

Focus on Results Rather Than Obsessing About Personal Image

Leaders often make the mistake of choosing image over substance. In his research, Collins (2001) discovered that the most effective leaders are humble, teachable, and tenaciously focused on fulfilling the main purpose of their organization's existence. He points out the fallacy of believing that dazzling celebrity-like leaders produce lasting change. The opposite is actually true. As he puts it, the most effective leaders are "plow horses, not show horses" (Collins, 2001, p. 20). Collins (2001) describes the most effective leaders as *level 5* leaders: people who are quietly and consistently committed to making the right choices again and again over a long period of time. It is important to keep this distinction of results versus charisma in mind for school leaders and messaging. The goal of messaging is not to portray an unrealistic perception of what is happening with students or teachers. The mission of your school must be based on results for students—the essential learning, growing, and developing happening in their minds and lives. Your messaging reinforces these outcomes by helping others see what is not always visible to those inside or outside of your school building.

Build Long-Term Momentum With Consistent Growth and Progress

Momentum is a powerful force, and when organizations consistently push toward common results, they begin to see their strengths grow exponentially. In other words, once long-term, consistent growth begins, it is hard to stop or slow it down. On the other hand, Collins (2001) warns against the *doom loop*—a pattern of constantly introducing new, radical changes that actually stall productivity and halt momentum. School leaders need to create an environment of consistent expectations, and these expectations need to be the focus of what you are communicating with others about your school. For instance, if the bulk of your email or face-to-face interaction is about announcements, calendar changes, or meeting times, then you are missing out on other ways to communicate about the long-term goals and progress of student learning in your school. But if the focus of your communication promotes the long-term objectives you share with teachers and students, then it is hard to stop those messages once the momentum begins.

Strong leaders understand their purpose, do the hard work, lead selflessly, and build momentum through consistency. If you're like me, that seems like a tall order. But be encouraged; no one leads perfectly. Studying good models, however, can help us avoid many of the pitfalls of distraction, self-promotion, and unnecessary changes. As you build a system of strong messaging for your school, you must keep in mind the essential elements that move organizations (including schools) from good ones to great ones.

Another characteristic of effective leaders is the ability to positively engage members of the community or organization, and messaging plays a strong role in your ability to engage others.

Show Leadership and Positive Engagement

Gallup's (2013) *State of the American Workplace* report analyzes one hundred million American workers and what makes them effective or ineffective in their work. The report shows how engagement practices play a significant role in job performance (Gallup, 2013). The following sections explore findings from Gallup's report that also apply to leaders of school communities.

Win Hearts and Minds

Gallup (2013) finds that to win customers—and a bigger share of the marketplace—companies must first win the hearts and minds of their employees. For education leaders, this means students, teachers, parents, and the community. This can only happen through engaging in relationships. No amount of communication will be effective unless leaders first understand their audience. Only when we are truly connected to the ideas, activities, and lives of our students, teachers, and families will they respect and be receptive to the messages we send on behalf of the school.

Use Management to Reduce Deficiencies

The Gallup (2013) report notes that the best-managed workplaces have nearly 50 percent fewer accidents and 41 percent fewer quality defects. You might ask how this statistic relates to education. It shows that deficiencies reflect directly on management; it is not a reach to think that schools would have a similar correlation. Consider how your school management directly affects the message you send about your school.

- Is your messaging positive and focused on the mission? Does it reflect the school culture you seek to build?

- Are you explaining (in writing, spoken words, gestures, and deeds) what you expect of students, teachers, and parents?

- Do you follow up regularly with reminders of goals, strategies, and outcomes?

- Do you reinforce in word and deed the values you want others to repeat?

- Do you hold accountable those who violate the shared mission and values of your school?

An experienced superintendent once told me that leading a school or a district is like managing a classroom (M. Bias, personal communication, June 15, 2004). When you approach it with the same preparation, planning, monitoring, and attention that a strong teacher shows, you will see good results. That commonsense advice goes a long way in any setting.

Accelerate Engagement

Gallup's (2013) study finds that organizations see improved results when they enact certain practices to accelerate engagement, such as selecting the right people for the team, developing employees' strengths, enhancing employees' well-being, and avoiding using only feel-good incentives.

Select the Right Team Members

The most important way we communicate to our students, staff, and parents the priorities we have for student learning is with the people we choose—teachers and other staff members—to lead and teach. Often when I interview a prospective teacher or staff member, I ask myself the question, "Is this someone I would want teaching my own child?" Keeping that perspective on staffing decisions helps you tie the mission of your school directly to the people serving students. And this serves as a great example when communicating with parents. For example, if you choose teachers with that question in mind, you can tell parents with confidence, "You can trust that this teacher is focused on your child's best interest." Messaging about great learning is so much easier when you have team members producing great learning. It is the school leader's responsibility to seek out and support the right team members.

Develop Strengths

Developing strengths in your team members, students, and parents means you are committed to recognizing and supporting the best characteristics in every member of the school community. Communicating these strengths happens in many ways—with specific feedback during daily interactions, with reflections from observations and evaluations, by celebrating successes, and by providing ongoing professional development.

For example, I once observed a mathematics teacher during an Algebra II class as he showed a video clip on a fascinating study involving chaos theory. The video itself was not directly tied to learning standards for Algebra II, but it provided an excellent hook for connecting students' learning to other applications beyond algebra. The teacher was helping students see how plotting numbers on a random sequence was actually not as random as expected. This use of hooking students with an interesting mathematics application was a strong instructional choice. I affirmed the choice by sharing a link of the video clip via email with all teachers along with an explanation of the teacher's lesson. By highlighting the strengths you see in someone else, you affirm what he or she is doing well, and you can inspire others to think about how to keep developing their own strengths.

Interestingly, nowhere in the study do Gallup (2013) researchers find a positive correlation between focusing on weaknesses and increased productivity. In fact, the opposite seems true: when you focus on the strengths of others, not the weaknesses, you inspire them to improve.

Enhance Well-Being

Promoting the well-being of those in your school involves a comprehensive approach to relationship building. Your messaging in this regard should be personal as well as organizational. With students or teachers, provide eye-to-eye contact and consistent feedback on successes and struggles to build relationships and stay connected. In addition, the kind of structures you create for schedules, calendars, and job descriptions should influence the kind of culture and environment that encourages, not discourages, positive well-being.

Avoid Using Only Feel-Good Incentives

During Teacher Appreciation Week, educators often receive many wonderful gifts from the school, parents, and members of the community. But if doughnuts, flowers, and other gifts are the only feel-good incentives the school provides, it has missed the mark for encouraging strong team engagement. The Gallup (2013) study finds that engaged employees are more motivated than those who simply work for perks or incentives. In other words, just because you commit to treating others like you want to be treated doesn't guarantee good performance. Schools are not for-profit institutions. And proponents of strategies like merit pay, for instance, often fail to understand the point of what makes a true incentive. The Gallup (2013) research asserts that engagement means giving people well-defined roles, helping them "make strong contributions," staying "connected to their larger team and organization," and "continuously progressing" (p. 28). In other words, people who understand the purpose of their work and find significant meaning in it derive motivation from it. Messaging cannot simply be built around feel-good moments. As important as those moments can be, you must also keep your communication centered on meaningful contributions and achievements—whether that is in individual conversations, group talks, or digital communication.

The Gallup (2013) report concludes with an amazing statistic:

> When organizations successfully engage their customers and their employees, they experience a 240% boost in performance-related business outcomes compared with an organization with neither engaged employees nor engaged customers. (p. 55)

The next time you gaze at a full moon, remember you are seeing only the side that is visible. As school leaders, we cannot always show others the full perspective we have of our school, but it is still our responsibility to attempt to try to show others as much of that perspective as possible. Can you imagine what kind of experience students, teachers, staff, and parents could have if they were fully engaged with the vision, mission, and goals of your school? This kind of engagement is only possible when leaders commit to a comprehensive approach to leadership and communication. Messaging must involve words, images, and digital tools, but it can't only include these things. Messaging must also enhance, celebrate, and support the strong practices of a school dedicated to achieving positive outcomes. Entire school communities can't reach these outcomes together if members do not engage with the message.

> ### Now It's Your Turn
>
> - When was the last time you reflected on the mission and vision of your school?
> - What goals are you moving toward where you see positive momentum building? How can you encourage messaging around those achievements and goals?
> - What steps are you taking to communicate high expectations?
> - What steps can you take to increase your own engagement and that of your teachers and school community?
> - Think about a classroom activity, student, or teacher who is modeling the main goals of your school. How can you share that story with your teachers, parents, and community?

Build a Foundation for Effective Communication

After spending eleven years in the classroom, nine years as an assistant principal, and four years as a high school principal, I have many varied experiences to reflect on when considering my career in education. When I think about my years teaching, I don't have a lot of regret about my curriculum decisions, although I always had room for improvement. And I don't feel regret for the duties or responsibilities I have managed in school administration, although I always have room for improvement there too. During reflection, any regret I feel almost always centers on times when differing perspectives caused conflict, misunderstanding, disagreement, or letdowns.

For example, when I was a classroom teacher, I once had a parent conference with a mother who told me that her son came home upset when I refused to give him credit for a test question he said he had marked correctly. When he brought the test to me, it appeared he had erased and rewritten the answer after I had passed back the test. I told him I couldn't give him credit at that point because it was too late for me to know whether he had corrected it after I passed it back or I had marked it incorrectly. His mother expressed that my assumption that the student had practiced academic dishonesty was crushing for him; he had great respect for me, and it hurt him that I did not trust him.

Now when I reflect on the situation, I can see both sides. This mother was not aware of my experiences in the classroom of observing students attempting to hide notes under their desks during assessments, or others who tried to share copies of tests with classmates via their mobile phones. I had gone over the answers with students after passing back the test because it is good instructional practice. I was a young teacher, however, and didn't think about asking students to put away their writing utensils while we reviewed their answers.

At the time, I'm sure I didn't think about how to address the situation with the student without seeming dismissive. It was likely a twenty-second interaction with a student that frankly I never thought about afterward until the mother brought it up. She explained it to me very politely—not because she wanted her son's points corrected but because she wanted me to know how much my opinion had mattered to him. When I think back to that situation now, twenty years later, I don't regret that I made a judgment call with the best information I had at the time. But I do regret that I was unaware of how powerful a twenty-second interaction could be with a student. The good news is that I took the mother's story to heart so that I became more mindful in my interactions with students. The bad news is that I may have made the same mistake a thousand times and not even noticed it.

What if we flip this scenario on its head? What if the power of positive interactions multiplied over and over again can create a momentum of strong culture in our schools? If you are making a commitment to better messaging with your students, teachers, and community, you must begin by understanding the characteristics necessary to positively engage school communities in order to see a more positive school culture taking shape. An integral component of such a culture is developing a foundation for effective communication in the following ways.

Be Trustworthy

This should go without saying, but in order for your messages to be trusted sources of communication, you must be trustworthy. No amount of planning, preparing, communicating, or accountability will be effective if you have not earned the trust of those who are listening to your messages. Building trust starts with building strong relationships, and it continues with reliable, consistent follow-through. When you've taken time to invest in relationships and given others the best information available, people are more forgiving. This is especially true when you can't show them both sides of the moon; many situations in school require privacy or confidentiality.

Begin by Listening

You can learn a lot by just listening. Taking time to listen and reflect with staff, students, and parents will strengthen your understanding of their perspectives. You will discover areas in which people need direction, guidance, or clarity and can answer their questions and better understand their interests. Schedule time to meet and listen, or collect feedback using surveys (such as the online platform SurveyMonkey, www.surveymonkey.com).

Listen for the Story Behind the Story

It would be difficult to find a school leader who has not heard teachers, students, and parents share their frustrations from time to time. When people share, they often make statements that include words like *always* and *never*. Even though people might seem to be simply venting with these statements, they often contain some important elements of truth. For example, it is easy to become offended when a teacher says, "We are asked to do too much with absolutely no support." Or a student might say, "My teacher *always* grades us unfairly." When you accept that such universal statements are common when people are frustrated, you can begin to listen for the story behind the story. What the student speaking about grades may really be saying, for example, is, "What I really want is for my teacher to recognize the value of my hard work, dedication, and commitment." By listening for the deeper meanings, leaders go to the other side of that person's moon to understand the messages he or she is communicating and what response or follow-up those messages require.

Don't Allow Misunderstanding to Keep You From Communicating

This may be one of the toughest lessons in leadership and in life. We all want others to understand and respect us. Others may never have access to the information you understand or the context in which you operate as they discuss issues with you.

For instance, a teacher who has asked to meet with you about a concern may have no idea that you just dealt with an intense situation involving bullying and harassment. You may have spent the previous thirty minutes calming an upset parent or finishing the forty-eighth page of your accreditation report. But you do not always have the luxury of explaining context when someone needs a moment to interact with you. Because others deserve our respect and attention, we cannot hold them hostage to whatever challenges or frustrations we are facing. So it is okay to accept that others can't see the side of the moon you are facing. And it's helpful to remember that they have areas you can't see either.

Try to See the Other Side

When was the last time you reflected on the influence your communication may be having on others? How is your messaging helping or hurting others in their attempt to have a better perspective?

You may be managing personnel decisions or implementing policies for student discipline, or you may be guiding choices on curriculum or instruction. Whatever the tasks ahead, don't forget that at the end of the day, the moments that matter most will often be the small moments. It may even be a twenty-second conversation—a word of encouragement you offer a teacher or student. Or maybe it's a reminder you give someone that he or she is talented and has something to offer the world. It may be a program you've helped develop.

No matter what pressures you face throughout your school, keep in mind that there are others whose lives are simply or sometimes radically influenced when they know you believe in them, want the best for them, and provide opportunities for them to learn.

We all want others to understand our point of view; however, you cannot allow your motivation to always achieve perfect understanding drive your messaging. Sometimes you can build stronger trust when you accept that you are limited in your perspective, when you must listen openly to learn from others, and when you give others the benefit of the doubt even when you can't always see the other side of every issue. When you acknowledge this perspective and begin communicating from it, it helps you see how you can still direct, coach, announce, guide, and celebrate common goals without being caught off guard by limited understanding.

Now It's Your Turn

- Do you make time to listen?

- What positive steps can you take to be a better listener?

- How comfortable are you with the knowledge that no matter how great your intentions or comprehensive your communication tools, others may sometimes misunderstand you?

- What steps are you willing to take to see the other side of the moon with your students, teachers, parents, and community?

Wrap Up

Successful leadership is not simply about focusing on evaluations, test scores, or wins and losses. Data are important, but leaders must see data as contributing factors to the overall positive culture and learning experiences. The implications of the Gallup (2013) research for school success are clear: engagement begins when we first create an environment in which students and staff members feel valued and heard, are engaged, understand what their roles are, and know what they can do to develop their strengths. They must also feel that their leader understands the foundation of effective communication. Once they are engaged, watch out! Your messaging within an engaged culture is much more than a set of words; it is a call to action.

Cultivating a Positive Message With Teachers

Communication is the key, and it's the one thing I had to learn. . . . I was so involved with the visual and technical aspects that I would forget about the actors.

—Steve Buscemi

As an actor, Steve Buscemi had the advantage of spending years in front of the camera before he began working behind the camera as a director. But like anyone who steps into a leadership position, he had to learn that management of others is not just about outcomes; it is ultimately about people. The same lesson applies in school leadership.

For several summers, I had the privilege of traveling to Washington, DC, as a coordinator for our state principal's association. One of my responsibilities was to set up educational advocacy meetings with members of Congress on Capitol Hill. One summer I traveled there with my superintendent of schools, Rick Thomas. On our last day in Washington, we had some downtime before heading to the airport. We decided to rent a kayak and paddle along the Potomac River to Theodore Roosevelt Island.

As we settled into our boat and started paddling, we quickly discovered we weren't making much progress. I was paddling in one direction while Rick was paddling in another. After realizing what we were doing, we laughed and then agreed that paddling *together* would be a lot more effective than each of us trying to separately navigate the course. As I paddled in front, and he provided steering in the rear, we finally began gliding across the water near the Key Bridge.

As this story shows us, when we paddle together—when we form a cooperative culture, collaborate, and communicate effectively—we achieve more than we could alone. Begin with a focus on these three Cs to help promote positive messaging with teachers in a school community.

Emphasize the Three Cs

There are some mindsets you can cultivate with the teachers and other staff members at your school so that you are paddling together throughout the school year. Each one plays a significant role in how well everyone steers in the same direction—not just on the first day of school but all year long.

Encourage a Cooperative Culture

Your messaging should encourage team members to embrace norms and shared practices that create a supportive learning culture in which teachers feel safe to teach and continue to learn. You model culture by the way you behave. When you greet teachers with phrases like, "Hi. How can I help you today?" or when you stop and give someone a moment of undivided attention, you create an environment where he or she feels safe to learn and teach. Nothing damages a school culture more than a climate in which teachers feel unsure, unsafe, or unproductive.

Your messaging must help teachers feel confident, safe, and productive. The first place this happens for many teachers is during the interview process. Interviewing is the perfect time to communicate the values, outcomes, and priorities you expect and provide. Another ripe moment for messaging is in your very first faculty meeting of the year. Just like a classroom teacher needs to immediately engage students, school leaders need to engage teachers in the expectations, procedures, and processes everyone shares to encourage a positive school environment. Then throughout the year, re-emphasize this expectation of cooperation in conversations, emails, professional development, or faculty meetings. Make sure faculty handbooks include common expectations. Each faculty meeting, highlight best practices you are seeing among teachers. Acknowledge and talk about successes happening in classrooms. And then support teachers by expecting and maintaining a schoolwide environment that is safe and conducive to learning.

I remember working with one talented young teacher who was feeling overwhelmed with his responsibilities and requested a meeting. He brought with him a list of almost a dozen items he wanted to discuss. I responded to each item by reassuring him that the solution would be one that had his best interest and the best interest of his students in mind. I reminded him that teaching is hard but it is also rewarding. We navigated through his concerns, talking for almost an hour. When the meeting ended, he crumpled up his notes and threw them in my trash can.

"Thanks," he said. "I can't believe how much better I feel just having time to talk."

Talking for an hour was a big commitment for both of us after a busy day of school, but that one hour of conversation provided weeks of relief from the stress and anxiety he had been facing.

Promote Collaboration

Professionals cannot grow their skills in strategy or procedure without collaborating. Your school might invest time in becoming a professional learning community (PLC; DuFour, DuFour, Eaker, Many, & Mattos, 2016), discuss how to target students in need of intervention, or organize data or test results as a team, so team meetings may be mandatory. Regardless if this is the case or not, collaboration must be meaningful. As a leader, you should encourage a culture of collaboration among the teachers in your school by embedding collaborative practices into the processes and procedures of your school. Some leaders create schedules that include additional or encore periods for teaming while others set up master schedules so that teachers can communicate as a team around common plans. Just as you celebrate student learning, be sure your messaging includes reminders for and celebrations of teacher collaboration.

One year as we were encouraging stronger collaboration among our teachers, I decided to show a TED Talk by Margaret Heffernan (2015), a businesswoman and consultant, who uses research by William Muir to inform others about what truly makes some groups more productive than others. Muir studied the productivity of laying hens by taking the most productive layers away from an existing flock and creating a "super flock" over six generations. Muir allowed another set of laying hens to proceed six generations without interference. He was interested in learning whether his super flock would outperform the normal, everyday laying hen.

At the end of Muir's research, the results surprised him. The normal laying hens were far more productive than the super chickens. Why? The chickens in the normal group functioned interdependently while chickens in the super group identified the other super chickens as threats and pecked one another almost to extinction; in fact, only a handful of super chickens remained. Heffernan uses the research to point to some false assumptions we often make about groupings. So often we believe that if you group the most talented, smartest, and gifted individuals together, you will inevitably have more productivity. The truth, however, is that productivity is tied to elements so much greater than intelligence or giftedness. Heffernan (2015), after studying productivity in teams, finds three characteristics that make up truly productive teams (the kinds of teams where people are supportive, challenging, and collaborative). She states:

> First of all, they [productive teams] showed high degrees of social sensitivity to each other. This is measured by something called the "reading the mind in the eyes test." It's broadly considered a test for empathy, and the groups that scored highly on this did better. Secondly, the successful groups gave roughly equal time to each other, so that no one voice dominated, but neither were there any passengers. And thirdly, the more successful groups had more women in them. (Heffernan, 2015)

Heffernan's important discoveries help communicate to teachers how important it is to keep growing collaboration skills. Here are some other ideas to cultivate better collaborative conversations at your school.

- Build in time for teachers to collaborate around common subject areas.

- Encourage teachers to collaborate around essential learning standards, outcomes, goals, and interventions.

- Encourage and support teachers who want to attend inspiring and educational workshops and conferences.

- Start a book club for staff members to discuss literature with a shared interest. For example, a principal friend of mine hosted a book study with his teachers to discuss Dave Burgess's book *Teach Like a Pirate* as a way to encourage conversations about strong instructional practices.

- Make it possible for new teachers to spend a day observing veteran teachers by hiring substitutes to cover classes.

Finally, you cannot expect collaboration unless you are a part of team meetings with teachers. In my building, we create data teams for teachers to track student essential learning skills. When I sit down with these teams, my main goal is to make sure that I understand how their students are learning. My secondary goal is to help teams demonstrate understanding of processes, clarify misunderstandings, or guide next steps. Being a part of these discussions means I am not just expecting but also modeling collaboration.

Strengthen Communication

Everyone loves good customer service; consider for a moment what it means to you. You probably think of a consistent, fair, friendly, and helpful environment. Everything about the company communicates this level of service. Now consider teachers as the customers. As a school leader, what could you do to communicate your intention to provide good customer service to your teachers?

- Be visible throughout your building. If you want teachers greeting students, you should model the behavior.

- Invite teachers to join you for conversations. Invite department or teacher leaders to meet with you before your next faculty meeting so you have their perspectives while building the upcoming meeting agenda.

- Be friendly and helpful in your communications.

- Respond to questions and concerns in a timely manner.

- Provide reassurance even when you have to say no to requests you can't satisfy.

- Provide regular updates on important issues. These updates can be emails with quick summaries of the week in review, upcoming events, and important reminders. This way, teachers don't have to wait until faculty meetings for consistent, helpful reminders on overall school procedures, expectations, and happenings.

- Maintain an office environment that reflects the kind of classroom environment you expect. Obviously, the two settings are different. But both should be professional, friendly, efficient, and student-centered.

To refer back to my earlier story, paddling on a river can be hard work. As my colleague and I worked together to move our kayak forward on the Potomac, we learned some valuable lessons about the importance of sending messages that encourage cooperation and collaboration. As you guide the messages that come from your school, remember that you cannot successfully accomplish big tasks alone. Don't forget that schools are built by people serving people, and this happens when you commit yourself to emphasizing the three Cs—cooperative culture, collaboration, and effective communication.

Now It's Your Turn

- What are your strengths and weaknesses in promoting the three Cs—cooperative culture, collaboration, and effective communication—among your teachers and staff?

- How do you and your staff paddle together? What is one step you can take each month to gather input from your staff to make sure you're paddling in the same direction?

Develop Key Responsibility Areas

Another way to cultivate a positive message with teachers is to develop key responsibility areas. The summer before I became a high school principal, I bought a copy of *EntreLeadership: 20 Years of Practical Business Wisdom From the Trenches* by Dave Ramsey (2011), a radio host, author, and speaker. In writing about how he manages the employees of his small business, he developed what he calls *key results areas* (KRAs) for each of his employees. These KRAs define employee results and help drive actions and outcomes (Ramsey, 2011). I started thinking about how Ramsey's KRAs could apply to school leadership and adapted them for my school with a slight change: *key responsibility areas*. These areas define teacher and staff responsibilities and facilitate collaboration and communication.

Key responsibility areas have been invaluable in our school. When leaders take time to define expectations with the entire staff from the beginning, they spend less time correcting and redirecting throughout the school year and more time watching others implement their well-defined roles. As a staff, we review the key responsibility areas together at the beginning of the year, adjust them as needed throughout the year, and add goals. We end each school year by reviewing them together again.

For example, the following lists are two examples of key responsibility areas developed with the staff members who manage office areas in my high school.

- Main Office Secretary
    - Maintain absense management and substitute website
    - Update accreditation notebook
    - Assist site principal
    - Build help desk items
    - Is the contact for alarms
    - Maintain budget spreadsheet
    - Keep inventories
    - Update Google calendar
    - Maintain purchase orders
    - Assist nurse with medications
    - Update school app
    - Maintain school calendar
    - Maintain school directory
    - Secure tech code updates
    - Keep teacher certification records
    - Maintain time sheets for hourly employees

- Registrar
  - Assist counselors and recruiters
  - Coordinate backpack food
  - Update dropout and transfer codes
  - Assess eligibility
  - Update end-of-instruction grades and test scores
  - Give locker assignments
  - Manage counselor schedules
  - Manage lists per requests
  - Complete new student enrollment paperwork
  - Produce progress report and report card printouts
  - Request records
  - Schedule conference rooms
  - Fulfill state-reporting data requests
  - Manage student records
  - Update transcripts

Key responsibility areas like these are built in team meetings so that staff members have input on their own responsibilities. Plus, sharing them with others ensures you are not unknowingly duplicating services. How do key responsibility areas affect messaging? One of the most important conversations to have when discussing key responsibility areas is about how each staff member should focus on customer service. Public schools are in the business of serving people. Key responsibility areas might at first look like simple lists of responsibilities; however, leaders must emphasize the importance of going beyond what's on paper to treat everyone with dignity and respect in all actions team members take—from answering the phone and greeting parents to working with colleagues, planning lessons, and interacting with students. Because we communicate often about expectations through written goals and conversations, leaders and teachers must share a common language in the collective messages they send the school community.

Model the Behavior You Expect From Teachers

Written messaging is very important, but messaging is about more than words. Leaders must model the behaviors and actions they expect from teachers. As this section explains, they must be teachable goal setters who are professional, have a good attitude, and always remember to celebrate.

Be Teachable

School leaders want their teachers to be team players, collaborators, and lifelong learners. It is important to model these same behaviors for your staff. Model and communicate through words and actions that you don't expect them to know it all, and that you encourage them to explore new solutions, methods, or knowledge. Keeping an open mind does not mean being gullible or open to manipulation. Instead it means staying humble and working with (not against) others to reach common goals. If you ever think there is no more to learn, it is time to find a new profession.

Jimmy Casas (2016), principal of Bettendorf High School in Bettendorf, Iowa, expresses this idea well in his blog post, "Wherever You Are Going, You Are Almost There." As a veteran leader of a model school, he reminds principals that they never stop learning:

> Simply put, no matter how many years we serve in the role of a school leader, we will never ever "get there." . . . As soon as you think you have it (whatever "it" is) figured out, the variable changes and the role of a school administrator quickly humbles you. (Casas, 2016)

A humble acceptance of lifelong learning keeps your focus on the perspective of others. One semester when our teachers were trying to develop a stronger remediation schedule, administration team members and I met with teacher teams throughout the building over a one-month period to ask them for feedback on ideas for a new schedule. Although we found great models that other schools used, it was important for our teachers to think through the pros and cons and provide input and solutions together. We even decided to beta test new schedule ideas the last semester of school in order to practice and test schedule samples for the coming school year. Your messaging throughout the process of leading new initiatives should involve face-to-face interactions, collaboratively built models, and debriefing meetings for feedback.

Be a Goal Setter

We ask students to set goals, so it makes sense to expect teachers to set goals as well. At the beginning of my second decade of working in schools, I decided I wanted to begin a blog in order to share ideas with school leaders. A number of teachers were working on master's degrees in school leadership, and they would often ask me the same questions about topics they were exploring for their classes and in their own practice. As a result, I set a goal to begin a blog and post at least once a week for the next five years. Later, I decided to add a podcast or audio version of my weekly posts. These goals required a lot of extra time after school hours, but I was committed to the goals for my own self-improvement as well as my desire to influence and inspire other school leaders to actions that would improve their service to schools. Three years into the journey, I was approached about publishing this book, expanding my options for sharing with others even farther beyond the walls of my school.

When you set higher goals for yourself, you can't help but see continuing improvement in your own learning, your platform for messaging, and in your service to others. And you cannot encourage teachers toward personal growth if you're not practicing it yourself.

Be Professional

We all have difficult days; despite this, it is important for leaders to model professionalism and to practice the common courtesies that we appreciate in and expect of others. Think before speaking, and disagree with respect and dignity. Come to school with your A game and permeate the school with the high expectations you want to see in your students. If you forget the essentials of common courtesy and professional behavior, others will not receive your messages with trust. In other words, when you fail to treat others with professional dignity, what you say falls on deaf ears.

Your messaging is never limited to the medium in which you publish, display, print, or send via technology. How you serve others is often your greatest message of all. For example, we have a procedure for teachers to sign in each morning, so I also sign in each morning. If you want teachers in hallways, in common areas, and at bus stops to safely supervise students, you must be there as well. When my superintendent or the state department needs reports from me in a timely manner, I plan accordingly—just as I expect others to do with deadlines for me.

Have a Good Attitude

Expect teachers to exhibit high standards, provide rigorous instruction, show strong people skills, and have a good attitude. As a leader, you should express this mindframe as well. One of the best examples of such an attitude comes from a former teacher in my building, Brooks Walton. Although he was in the classroom for more than twenty-five years, Mr. Walton consistently modeled a positive attitude. When you asked him, "How are you today?" his response was always, "I'm just living a dream!" And he meant it. One year as student council advisor, he helped sponsor the state student council convention, which brought thousands of students to our community for three days of meetings and activities. On the second morning of the convention, I saw Mr. Walton in the hallways an hour before school began. He had been up half the night preparing for activities, and his eyes were bloodshot. "Mr. Walton, are you okay?" I asked. "Yes," he said, looking up with a grin. "I'm just living a dream!" Mr. Walton's attitude was just as contagious when he taught creative lessons, created homemade videos in which he would rap, or helped organize schoolwide events. One year after his retirement, he passed away. So many people in our school community had been touched by his wit, creativity, and inspiration that they petitioned our school board to rename a building in his honor.

Remember to Celebrate

Finally, we cannot forget to celebrate. Jon Gordon is a motivational author and speaker who talks a lot about team building. I like Gordon's (2013) advice, "Each night before you go to bed complete the following statements: I am thankful for _____. Today I accomplished _____." These same statements apply to teachers and school leaders. Encourage teachers to reflect on what is working well, and where they want to grow. Great work also deserves great praise. When I meet with teachers after formal observations, I will often ask, "What do you believe is going well in your classroom? Where would you like to grow? What is something you want me to know?" I also take time to praise them in the areas where they are excelling before I coach them in areas where they may want to improve. In addition, I take time to email or post stories, photos, or highlights of great happenings throughout the school. This is when messaging becomes such a powerful tool. As you share, share, and share some more with others about the success of your colleagues, you build momentum for more great work. Be thankful together for the small wins and the big ones. When you commit to celebrating the positives in your school, you will ultimately overwhelm the negatives that so easily distract from great outcomes.

Now It's Your Turn

- How can you work to define key responsibility areas for the teachers in your school?

- Do you model the behaviors you expect from others in your school?

- In what ways can you make celebration a ritual for your teachers?

Provide Helpful Feedback

Cultivating a positive message also includes providing helpful feedback. Consider the following example. All of my children learned to swim with the help of two retired teachers who lived in our community. Ms. Suzanne was a kindergarten teacher, and Mr. Rick was a secondary teacher, coach, and principal. One day I was sitting poolside watching them teach a group of first and second graders. Ms. Suzanne was clear with instructions and enthusiastic about the lesson. Mr. Rick modeled and demonstrated the skills they were teaching. And they guided students through practice, correcting them when needed, and praising them when they succeeded. I remember thinking how I would have loved to film the entire session and share it as an example of great teaching. I love to swim, and I love to swim with my children. But Ms. Suzanne and Mr. Rick taught my children more than I ever could about swimming. They learned survival skills and techniques for each kind of stroke. And most of all, they learned to love the water. They had a deeper understanding of the content and skills of water safety and swimming than I possessed. But even though I was not as proficient as they were in understanding swimming techniques and strokes, I was able to identify their strong instructional practices.

When I was a language arts teacher, I understood the standards, strategies, and curriculum goals high school students needed to master in language arts. I taught students to effectively think, write, speak, and read. But when I transitioned to becoming a school administrator, I began observing and evaluating teachers from other subject areas—many vastly different from the one in which I had taught. Sometimes it can be intimidating to provide feedback to someone with a different area of expertise. But just as I could identify the excellent teaching abilities of our swim instructors, I have learned to see the characteristics of successful and struggling teachers in any subject. Being able to identify the positive qualities of good instruction is an important role in school leadership. Paying close attention to these positives helps you craft encouraging messages as you support a positive school culture and maintain enthusiasm for good teaching and learning. Feedback should focus on sending the message that learning is what matters most and that collaborating is a priority.

Remember That Learning Is What Matters Most

Each year, before school even begins, my assistant principals and I schedule the time we will spend in classrooms. We identify the number of teachers we can formally observe and evaluate each week. We share the schedules in advance so that teachers know in which windows of time to expect visits and follow-up meetings. By planning what matters most—the monitoring of effective teaching and learning—in advance, leaders can then schedule other events and meetings around classroom observation times. Giving teachers these schedules in advance sends a clear message that student learning is the priority around which school leaders build their scheduled times in classrooms.

In addition, spending time with teachers and students in their learning environment provides you with an endless supply of good news to share with others about your school. You have direct contact with students and can discover where teachers need help, how they are growing, and if they may need more resources. Taking a role and being visible in the classroom reinforces a leader's role as chief communicator as well as the teacher's role as an instructional leader.

Remember That Collaborating Is a Priority

Leaders must take responsibility for prioritizing reflection and discussion time for instructional strategies. Teachers need this team time to talk more deeply about student learning with others who share the same focus (grade level or subject). In teams, teachers share best practices, discuss what works for them, and examine results from student data. They can set goals for instructional outcomes and share remediation strategies. Encouraging collaboration sends a strong message to teachers that feedback is critical to improved instruction, and that you and their peers are committed to finding ways to improve teacher and student performance. School leaders send a strong message that collaboration is the priority when they plan far in advance for times of team building. When you are building a master schedule, for instance, keep in mind which teachers need common planning periods or what kind of remediation schedule promotes focused times of reteaching. You cannot simply talk about collaboration; instead, you must structure time and plan the schedule so that teachers have the opportunity for collaboration.

Identify and Encourage Positive Instructional Behaviors

When seeking to cultivate a positive message with teachers, consider what kinds of instructional behaviors you identify and encourage through your messaging, regardless of the academic subject. Take a look at the observation and evaluation structures you have in place. My high school uses the Teacher Leader Effectiveness model (TLE) for teacher observations and evaluations (Tulsa Public Schools, 2015). This model identifies categories of teacher behavior that leaders can observe and encourage in teachers, regardless of the subject area. For example, the TLE model identifies twenty categories that measure teacher effectiveness (Tulsa Public Schools, 2015).

1. **Preparation:** Teachers are ready for student learning with materials, technology, and processes well prepared to optimize the best learning environment.

2. **Discipline:** Teachers have established expectations. They are communicating with students in ways that demonstrate mutual respect.

3. **Buildingwide climate responsibility:** Teachers are committed to a culture of consistency and accountability throughout the entire school, not just in the classroom.

4. **Lesson plans:** Lessons identify essential learning standards and match curriculum maps. Teachers collaborate with others for planning and tracking student achievement.

5. **Assessment practices:** Teachers measure learning with consistent, immediate feedback for students.

6. **Student relations:** Teachers establish positive rapport with students by modeling the kinds of behaviors they expect students to demonstrate.

7. **Literacy:** Student learning is tied to consistent practices in reading, writing, speaking, and analysis. Students are engaged with learning through written expression.

8. **Current state standards:** Curriculum maps and lesson plans reflect essential learning standards that align with state requirements.

9. **Involvement of all learners:** Students are engaged in the learning process. Teachers draw distracted or disconnected students back into meaningful learning.

10. **Explained content:** Explanations are clear and concise. Teachers re-explain content to clarify student misunderstanding.

11. **Clear instruction and directions:** Processes, transitions, and directions are clear to students. Teachers take time to make sure students understand before moving on in a lesson.

12. **Modeling:** Teachers demonstrate the skills or learning for students. They use examples to help improve student understanding.

13. **Monitoring:** Teachers are visible and moving around the room. They interact with students to ensure learning is taking place.

14. **Adjustment based on monitoring:** If misunderstanding occurs, teachers are flexible in adjusting lessons or reteaching content.

15. **Closure established:** Teachers take time to assess student learning at the end of a lesson, repeat main points, and set the stage for what is coming next.

16. **Student achievement:** Teachers regularly inform students of how they are performing or achieving in their learning. Teachers use student data as a way to track or analyze learning or growth.

17. **Professional development:** Teachers are involved in continuing education the district provides or engaged in training outside of the district.

18. **Professional accountability:** Teachers meet expectations for deadlines, reports, grades, or other required duties or responsibilities.

19. **Effective interpersonal skills:** Teachers communicate and collaborate with one another. They provide positive and meaningful feedback to parents or other members of the school community.

20. **Professional involvement and leadership:** Teachers are role models or mentors for others in their own professional behavior.

Obviously, no one practices these behaviors perfectly. But setting these common expectations as a part of the observation process reinforces the kind of message leaders want to consistently communicate about student learning. What I like about the model is that it focuses on performance and quality of education, not just on content. The categories help leaders identify positive teacher actions to reinforce and promote.

For example, when I make a formal observation, I spend the first twenty to thirty minutes observing without even looking at a rubric. I want to understand the dynamics of what is happening, get a sense for student interaction, and make sure I grasp the context of the lesson. I also check curriculum maps or lesson plans. After I've taken notes on those observations, I begin using a rubric that provides categories for what I have observed or still need to see.

Tulsa Public Schools (2015) uses a rubric that organizes the twenty TLE categories into five areas. Leaders rate and evaluate teachers on a scale from 1 to 5 (1 = ineffective; 2 = needs improvement; 3 = effective; 4 = highly effective; and 5 = superior) for each category. The organization is as follows.

- Classroom management (worth 30 percent of the total score). This section includes the following categories:

  1. Preparation
  2. Discipline
  3. Buildingwide climate responsibility
  4. Lesson plans
  5. Assessment practices
  6. Student relations

- Instructional effectiveness (worth 50 percent of the total score). This section includes the following categories:

  7. Literacy
  8. Current state standards
  9. Involvement of all learners
  10. Explained content
  11. Clear instruction and directions
  12. Modeling
  13. Monitoring
  14. Adjustment based on monitoring
  15. Closure established
  16. Student achievement

- Professional growth and continuous improvement (worth 10 percent of the total score). This section includes the following categories:

  17. Professional development
  18. Professional accountability

- Interpersonal skills (worth 5 percent of the total score). This section includes the following category:

  19. Effective interpersonal skills

- Leadership (worth 5 percent of the total score). This section includes the following category:

  20. Professional involvement and leadership

As you are formulating feedback for teachers, here is a summary of questions any rubric should help you answer.

- How does the teacher organize his or her instructional time to optimize learning experiences?
- How does the teacher connect today's lesson to prior learning or prompt students to consider the meaning or reasoning in today's lesson?

- Does the teacher clearly present the lesson, provide examples, and connect to prior learning?

- How does the teacher engage the students? Does he or she invite them to participate by reading aloud, working in groups, managing hands-on activities, writing responses, or experimenting in labs?

- What kind of monitoring, modeling, reteaching, and feedback does the teacher provide for students?

- What kind of prior planning and mapping has the teacher done before today's lesson?

- In mapping or planning, has the teacher identified skills in line with state or college-ready curriculum standards?

- What kind of professional behavior, outreach to parents, leadership among staff and teachers, or professional development has this teacher been pursuing?

- How does the teacher modify for and accommodate students with special needs?

- How does the teacher summarize and assess student progress? How does the teacher check for student learning and reiterate the main lessons learned today?

It is important to follow up observations in a timely manner with the teacher, reviewing and discussing the feedback. During these meetings, I ask questions like, "Where do you feel things are going well, and where do you see room for improvement?" or "What are some ways I can better support what you're doing?" Some teachers need clear direction if they are unaware of ways to improve, but most teachers have a keen sense of their own strengths and weaknesses, and reflecting together allows them to be a part of finding solutions or resources and ask for more specific feedback.

Another way you can identify and reinforce quality instruction is by asking students to explain what they're learning. Many times they can explain it in easy-to-understand terms that help you form follow-up questions. If you ask students these questions with a teacher nearby, the teacher can follow up with more explanation or clarify misunderstanding. Finally, student performance can help you gauge effectiveness. Keep it simple: Can the student demonstrate what he or she just learned? How are the majority of students scoring on exit exams? In future settings, do students require significant remediation, or do the majority perform at appropriate levels? With these thoughts in mind, how do you communicate feedback to their instructors? How do you publish and celebrate the wonderful instruction that is happening in your building?

If you want to send strong messages about student learning, you must first set the stage by communicating those expectations. No matter how long you have practiced a skill, you always have room to grow in your own performance. Likewise, you usually know a great performance when you see it. Just like I could identify the effective instruction that my children's swim instructors provided, you can identify effective teaching and best practices—regardless of the age level or subject matter—when you look for the skills, enthusiasm, feedback, and outcomes that students most commonly display when they are achieving at high levels. Then you have even more reason to celebrate learning and continually communicate to your teachers the message that their teaching matters. Whether you're enjoying observing the skills of swim instructors or the insights of a biology teacher, you can learn to identify and celebrate strong instruction in any setting.

Now It's Your Turn

- What are some ways you've learned to identify strong instruction and provide helpful feedback to others, regardless of their subject matter?

- Share some best practices by asking other school leaders for practical ways they schedule time in classrooms or communicate to others that learning matters.

Wrap Up

When sixty-four-year-old world-record swimmer Diana Nyad crawled onto the sandy shores of Florida after achieving her dream of swimming one hundred miles from Cuba, journalists surrounded her trying to catch a good quote. When they asked her to comment on her amazing accomplishment, she barely had strength to talk. But she said two things. One, *never ever give up*. And, two, *teamwork* (Nyad, 2013). Nyad was not just a solitary figure swimming the ocean blue. She swam the distance, but she was also surrounded by boats full of specialists in navigation, fitness, nutrition, and rescue. She never gave up, and she needed others to help her achieve her dream.

You may not face attacking jellyfish in your messaging with others, but you will confront some tough challenges. Whether it is a tough student, a difficult parent, or a new policy to implement, you will encounter rough waters every day. But you will also experience some great successes. No matter what challenges you face, determine to finish strong together by staying committed to the all-encompassing power of good messaging. Communicate ahead of time your expectations, decide on your shared values, target your strategies, and commit to your goals. When the entire trajectory of your school is in a positive direction, then your messaging will carry the weight of integrity and trust.

Using Strategies for Positive Messaging With Teachers

Electric telegraph [communication] will never be a substitute for the face of someone who with [his or her] soul encourages another person to be brave and true.

—Charles Dickens

Most of us have heard the story about the married couple in which the wife is a strong communicator and the husband is the silent type. One day the wife asks the husband, "Honey, do you still love me?"

"Well," he says, looking up from his newspaper, "I told you twenty-five years ago that I love you. And I haven't changed my mind since then."

As this lighthearted story shows, you can't assume that since you've communicated something one time that the recipient remembers the message. Chief communicators in schools must always strive to grow and learn, adding more ideas to their toolkits for improving school messages with teachers and staff. This chapter offers strategies for positive messaging, technology strategies, strategies for meaningful feedback, and strategies for facilitating change.

Employ Strategies for Positive Messaging

As a principal, I often meet with other local educators. Once the head of an education graduate program was driving by our school and decided to stop in for an unannounced visit. Unfortunately, I was in a meeting at the time. She left a note with our front office secretary. In the note, she said, "Sorry I was unable to see you, but I wanted to let you know you have a beautiful school, and your office staff was welcoming, friendly, and helpful." First impressions only happen once, and although you have many opportunities to communicate positive messages, you can never underestimate the power of how others perceive your school. In addition to having staff and teachers who share and promote the positive values of your school, consider implementing some of the following tools to enhance your positive communication.

Establish Spirit Builders

Start the school year off right by promoting community building among staff members and sending the message that your school is a positive and supportive environment. One tradition we have established to capture the energy and excitement of a new school year is for our student council leadership and teachers to collaborate on creating a staff logo and T-shirt. Over the summer, our student council sponsor solicits feedback from administration, teachers, and student leaders on ideas for an annual theme. For instance, one year we used the theme "Stay PoweRED up!"—a play on words with our school color. We start the year with an annual photo shoot where staff members sport their shirts for the first time. They continue to wear the shirts every Friday throughout the school year. We have found that local vendors have been willing to donate shirts for our school, and our local school foundation, the Skiatook Public School Support Foundation, once provided a grant to cover shirt costs for the entire district. This type of involvement allows the community to share in the spirit as well. Sharing and posting photos from the first staff meeting both in the school and in community publications adds to the message that we are a unified instructional community.

Introduce and Continue Traditions

Traditions are powerful motivators for a positive culture. One of our traditions includes handing out a teacher-of-the month award. In addition, one veteran teacher at our high school, Brooks Walton, began a tradition of handing out an award at the end of each faculty meeting to acknowledge a teacher or staff member who had done something funny, embarrassing, or memorable. Soon after Mr. Walton's retirement, he passed away. He was so loved by our community, that the school board named a building in his honor. And we have continued the tradition of handing out a monthly award in his honor. So in addition to a teacher of the month, we also have a Brooks Walton Award recipient. One month, our staff volunteered to help set up vendor tables at a community festival. One of the vendors pulled up to the event with a trailer of animals, including a donkey. Somehow the teacher who was the most uncomfortable with animals ended up holding the donkey by a rope while the vendor set up his area. This turned into a funny moment with lots of photo opportunities, and later that month, the teacher received a Brooks Walton award for "Most Eager Animal Lover." What are some traditions that your teachers practice that encourage team building and make school a place they enjoy working?

Organize Celebrations

Organizing and promoting celebrations sends the message that you have a strong positive culture that values teachers. Each month we buy cookies or pastries to place in our teachers' lounge to honor teachers who have had birthdays. We bring doughnuts to every faculty meeting as a way to provide a breakfast treat for coming early to school. Holding a teacher appreciation week is one way to communicate to teachers and the entire community that you value a positive culture. A staff member at our school started a community campaign to solicit donations for Teacher Appreciation Week.

First, she drafted a brief but direct inquiry letter to inform potential partners about the event and articulate what donations she desired. Figure 3.1 (page 44) shows a sample letter. Then school office staff chose to deliver the letters by hand to local residents and businesses. They scheduled three days with two-hour blocks of time after lunch to canvas our community with requests for support. They asked for items like gift cards, donations for meals for teachers, or office supplies teachers could use in classrooms. Some in the community donated on the spot and others called back after a few days of thinking how they could help. Use follow-up conversations as a way to connect with potential donors, remind participants, or collect donations.

Dear Neighbor,

The Skiatook High School office staff is gearing up for the 2016 Teacher Appreciation Week in May! It is the time of year to honor and appreciate our teaching staff here at Skiatook High School. We are asking for your help to make it a year to remember. This year we are asking you to consider a donation to the Skiatook High School Bulldog teachers. Your donation will be greatly appreciated and will go to showing our teachers they matter. Please fill out the bottom of this form and list the items or dollar amount you are donating.

Thank you for your support of Skiatook High School teachers!

Name: _____

Phone: _____

Address: _____

Email: _____

Total amount donated: _____

Items donated: _____

Please return all donations to Skiatook High School or mail to 355 South Osage, Skiatook, OK 74070. If you have any questions, please email us or call at 918.396.1790.

Source: © 2017 Skiatook High School. Reprinted with permission.

Figure 3.1: Sample partner letter for teacher appreciation donations.

During the weeklong celebration, we hung a large banner in the school to honor the teachers. Many donors contributed food, which allowed us to have two breakfasts and two luncheons for teachers with items like biscuits and gravy, fruit trays, juice, doughnuts, and sandwiches.

More than thirty area businesses donated gift cards, T-shirts, services, and treats. So each day, as a part of our daily announcements, we drew names of teachers to win the donated goods. Spreading prize announcements, breakfasts, and luncheons throughout the week made the entire celebration fun and eventful. Of course, gratitude must follow generosity. It's important for leaders to send thank-you cards to generous friends in the community highlighting their kindness and support.

Whatever appreciation traditions you enjoy, be sure that you communicate throughout the entire process of showing appreciation, whether that's sharing announcements, emails, posts, or photos. Your goal is to continually communicate the message to staff, students, and the community that you value teachers in your school or district for the great work they do.

These strategies for positive messaging are a fun way for school leaders to reinforce and communicate a supportive school culture. Other strategies that support the day-to-day work of teachers, like technology strategies, also signal that you value a healthy and supportive culture.

Apply Technology Strategies

I have a twenty-five minute commute to work each day. During the drive to school, my sophomore daughter rides beside me in a sleepy daze. Most mornings, I listen to news, music, or a podcast on the way to school. When I pull my car into the parking lot, I unlock the front doors of the school, turn on the lights in the commons, and then unlock the doors to the main office before entering my code in the panel that disengages the security alarms. One day, I counted the number of doors I unlock before entering my office. I unlock ten doors.

Most of my students, teachers, and parents have no idea how many doors I unlock each morning at the start of the day. The same can be said about technology. Most people do not think about the different means by which they receive communication. But there are a lot of different "doors" that we can use to communicate. Technology provides many tools that can enhance the ways we communicate or send messages. Consider implementing some of the following technology tools to support a culture of collaboration and community.

Accomplish Work and Share Online

Some of the most practical tools a school faculty can use to support a culture of collaboration and community are those that make working and sharing online possible, such as Google Docs (https://docs.google .com) and Google Forms (https://docs.google.com/forms). Whether by sharing master schedules, class sponsor lists, or budget accounts, you can create an environment where teachers and staff have constant access.

Google Docs provide a place where any staff member can access resources and work collaboratively with his or her team members. Google Forms is a great way to collect data from one another; the creator of the form has the ability to move the data into one spreadsheet for analysis. Users only see the Google Form, but the creator can access all the data from the forms submitted. This a great way to collect ideas, surveys, numbers, or feedback from individuals that you can then convert into a document for analysis or record keeping.

For example, our teachers use Google Forms to enhance the way we collaborate on data teams. As teachers give common formative assessments, they enter student scores in shared Google spreadsheets that have tabs for each teacher by class period. Categories automatically populate based on which students are advanced, proficient, close to proficiency, or far from proficiency.

Another way use Google Docs is at the start of each school year. One member of our office staff creates a student count Google Form that she shares with the entire teaching staff. Teachers enter the number of students physically present in each class. These numbers automatically populate a linked Google Doc spreadsheet, which the office staff member can access. We have found this an easy and efficient way to collect counts throughout the building so that we can compare actual students present with students on our rosters to see who has not reported to school yet, who may have moved, or whose status we need to explore.

Use Video Files to Communicate

Throughout my career, there have been times when I needed to communicate important information to staff members, but I was unable to gather them all into one place at one time. One time, for example, our teachers were staying late for parent-teacher conferences. We had a meeting on the schedule, and I knew that bringing them into a meeting would only add more stress to an already busy schedule. At times such as these, leaders must be innovative. Using the built-in camera and microphone on my laptop, I have recorded video clips to send to staff, along with an agenda and notes. Because I value a culture where we respect each other's time, I decided to email a video clip of important information teachers needed to know. I keep the videos relatively short. I write a script ahead of time with bullet points so I remember all the critical points I need to cover. I only create these kind of clips in special circumstances, but when I do, I give teachers permission to skip watching the video if my notes are sufficient. However, I usually receive more responses from faculty about videos than I do when I share information in a text-based way. I don't use video clips often, but when I do, teachers seem to realize the information is important if I've taken the time to create a video.

If you're interested in creating a video clip, plan the agenda in advance as you normally would (create an agenda, draft handouts, list people to recognize, and so on). Then use a program to create the video, such as Microsoft Moviemaker or iMovie, with your webcam. After you are finished recording, upload the video to a video-sharing service such as YouTube for easy sharing. Be sure to use a private setting and then provide the link in your message to make the video accessible to your recipients.

Figure 3.2 is a sample email to teachers for a video faculty clip with an agenda. Visit https://youtu.be/Ql7iaR-ABrs to see a sample video clip I created for my teachers and staff.

Dear Staff,

Because we have a busy day tomorrow with parent conferences, I'm trying something new. We will have a faculty video in place of our usual meeting since there is a lot we need to share. Please follow these three steps for the video.

1. Watch the short video (https://youtu.be/Ql7iaR-ABrs) during your planning time or after school. Do not watch the video in front of students because I discuss teacher-only information. Here's the meeting agenda.
    A. A–F grade update
    B. Test scores
    C. SMART goal discussion
    D. Special needs document review: ten tips
    E. Parent conference reminders
    F. Teacher of the month
    G. Brooks Walton awards

2. Sign in tomorrow in the main office on the regular sign-in sheet and on the faculty meeting sign-in sheet so I know you have watched the video. Be sure to pick up your complimentary breakfast doughnuts when you sign in!

3. Congratulate our teachers of the month and Brooks Walton award winners who I identify at the end of the video.

Figure 3.2: Sample faculty video email and agenda.

I still prefer face-to-face meetings because of the opportunity to gauge feedback and connect in person. But busy times call for creative measures, and creative messaging draws attention to important communication and keeps everyone informed as vital members of the community.

Send Friday Follow-Ups

One assistant principal began a very effective tradition of reaching out to teachers (J. McElyea, personal communication, September 9, 2016). Each week, the administrative team discusses the highlights of the week and upcoming calendar items for the next week. On Fridays, teachers receive a Friday follow-up email with quick touch points from the meeting for them to remember going forward. Figure 3.3 shows an email from the assistant principal to our high school staff.

Good afternoon!

I hope everyone has had a great week! For next week, let's keep the following in mind.

- All curriculum maps should be updated for the new school year and used in instruction. If you still need to update your map, please do so as soon as possible.
- Next week is homecoming week! Mrs. Franklin will be sharing more information about hallway and door decorations.
- As excited as we all are about homecoming, we still need to maintain classroom structure and productive learning environments. Continue to press on with instruction and limiting time students are out of class.
- There will be some flexibility in dress code next week since dress-up days are planned. If you have concerns or questions about a student's outfit, refer him or her to administration so we can determine next steps.
- Finally, I can't end this week without a shout-out to our cafeteria staff. They have been extremely shorthanded this week. On top of that, their floor cleaning machine is down, which means they are mopping the entire commons area by hand! So, special thanks to them for feeding all of us and keeping the commons area looking great!

Have a great weekend!

Figure 3.3: Example of a Friday follow-up email.

Keep Six Quick Tech Tips in Mind

Technology can also be a powerful for tool for teacher communication. Here are six other ways a school leader can connect with teachers or encourage a culture of learning.

1. **Carry an iPhone or camera to capture moments:** Assuming your students and parents have authorized sharing images of students per Federal Educational Records Privacy Act of 1974 guidelines, you should be capturing and sharing positive moments every day of teachers in action from your school. Snap photos or take short videos of classroom activities, and then email them, post them, tweet them, or whatever it takes to have others see and celebrate great moments. For example, we shared four congratulations emails on teams or individuals who won awards or recognitions for drama, National Honor Society, Future Farmers of America, and choir. All of this, and it was just Monday when these were announced!

2. **Increase your social media shares**: If your district allows Facebook, Twitter, Instagram, or LinkedIn, then spread the news. These social media outlets are free publicity for the great happenings among your teachers. And your tech-savvy parents (which more and more of them are) will be thrilled to see what's happening at school, and they will often share it with their friends.

3. **Boost a post for more exposure:** During one semester, one of my teachers emailed some photos of positive notes students had left on a bathroom mirror. Soon this turned into a movement where girls were adding so many positive notes that the entire area became a "wall of kindness." We decided to spend five dollars and boost a post via Facebook on the wall of kindness our students started. As a result, that single post had more than sixty-five thousand impressions (the number of times it is seen). It's worth sharing great moments among your teachers and staff. Sometimes these same messages can be shared with audiences beyond your own school community.

4. **Share weekly summaries of great happenings**: For four years, we have shared a weekly newsletter with our parents. Most of the content for this newsletter comes from teachers, coaches,

and sponsors who are doing amazing work with students. Every week the newsletter includes highlights, photos, and summaries of the past week in review. Celebrating these great moments keeps everyone informed and encourages a momentum of consistent positivity.

5. **Use media relationships to promote teacher and student activities:** Make friends with your media outlets. Our local newspaper editor is cc'd on every email I send to teachers congratulating a student, teacher, or program on success. Once she told me that summers are her slowest time of year because school is out and those posts are on vacation as well. The same applies with TV or radio stations. Many of my teachers have followed suit and now include media outlets when emailing good news of classroom or activity successes. Sometimes when you send them a heads-up on great events, they will want to come to your school to share the good news.

6. **Push out press releases beyond your own community:** Since I have begun blogging, I have found an easy platform for highlighting great activities teachers and students are accomplishing. Sharing beyond your community brings outside attention that can be encouraging too. One way to do this is by taking advantage of bragging via other outlets like blogging, podcasting, Twitter, Facebook, and LinkedIn. Anytime you can brag about your teachers, students, and schools only adds to the positive environment you want to cultivate for strong learning and culture.

One of the ways we have increased our ability to use social media is by having a tech-saavy library assistant who loves updating social media platforms for our school. Anytime a teacher or administrator emails an update or photo of student learning or activity, she will update our school Facebook or Twitter platforms by duplicating the content there as well.

Even with the many ways we have learned to enhance communication through technology, one of my errors in the past was relying too heavily on my written or electronic communication with teachers for personal communication. Use technology to enhance your messaging, but remember that for personal feedback, nothing replaces meaningful face-to-face dialogue.

As you look at ways to communicate with your teachers, don't make the mistake the husband in the story that opened this chapter made of believing that others remember your ideas, messages, or words just because you've said them once already. Think about ways to constantly promote your ideas, show appreciation, and communicate important information.

Now It's Your Turn

- How do you currently promote positive messaging in your school, and in what ways could you further support a positive culture with teachers and staff?

- Think about one message you want to make sure teachers understand every week. How can you consistently redeliver that message in a new way to keep everyone moving in the same direction?

- Remember you're not in this alone. Who else on your team can you lean on to help broadcast, celebrate, or repeat important messages?

Practice Strategies for Providing Meaningful Feedback

I recognize a good golfer when I see one. He or she is usually the one who gets the ball in the hole with the fewest strokes. One observation I've made about great golfers, however, is that most of them have had a coach. Teaching is often a solitary profession. Teachers may interact with hundreds of students on a daily basis, but they are often the lone adult in the room. The way leaders communicate with and coach teachers is important. What kind of messaging are you sending the teachers you observe and evaluate?

A teacher in my school once shared with me her genuine disappointment in my lack of meaningful conversation and follow-through after observing her classroom. Although I had formally observed her teaching, I hadn't given her helpful feedback. I knew then that I had to commit to prioritizing time for feedback. Here are some of the strategies I implemented.

Be Visible

Whether it is before school or between classes, teachers want to know their school leaders are present to support them. Especially at the start of each school year, I make it a point to walk through every classroom to welcome back teachers and see students face to face. Also, I schedule meetings in every high school English class so that I can talk to students face to face about goals, guidelines, and expectations. Teachers have commented to me how they appreciate the direct feedback so that students see the common values we are sharing among the adults in our building.

Attend Team Meetings

Our high school data teams meet every week. Whether a teacher is in a subject area that matches content with another teacher or if he or she is a singleton subject area, every teacher is a part of some kind of team. Meeting in person with teams is important even if I am not the one responsible for running the meeting. The face-to-face interaction provides time for reflection and feedback. We share the data we cover via Google Docs so that we can maintain conversations over student progress even when we are not physically in the same room.

Invite Teachers to Leadership Lunches

Once a month, I host a time in my office during our lunch periods for department heads or anyone else interested in leadership discussions about our school. These conversations provide valuable feedback from teachers on areas that are priorities for them. Normally, these conversations build agendas for upcoming faculty meetings as well.

Attend Events and Games

When coaches or sponsors invest hours of each day toward helping students with activities or events, they want to know they are supported and valued. Being at their events or games help students see that we all value their performance. It also reminds teachers we see and appreciate their hard work too.

Schedule a One-Week Observation Range

Another strategy I use when planning teacher observations is scheduling visits to occur during a designated one-week period, rather than on a specific day. The advantage of scheduling in advance within a one-week period is that teachers know the observation will occur—it shouldn't be a surprise—and it provides flexibility for the teacher to communicate about times to avoid observation, like during a class period when students are testing. Scheduling the one-week range also allows flexibility if an unexpected shift in schedule is necessary.

Make Observing the Priority

When visiting classrooms, if you're like me, you may be tempted to immediately begin checking off all the boxes on an observation form. But don't forget the most important reason you're there—to give meaningful feedback. Resist the urge to simply complete a task; instead, remember to make watching, listening, and learning priorities, and then complete formal notes.

Give Effective Feedback

If you spend significant time in a classroom, always follow up with teachers with written feedback or follow up face to face. Although you should share observation forms with teachers, the forms cannot be the end goal of the interaction; instead, forms are simply tools to reinforce suggestions, redirect if needed, lead into questions, and reinforce compliments.

Leaders can give feedback in many ways: sometimes I send a quick email explaining something specific I saw a teacher doing that was noteworthy. For instance, I once emailed a special education teacher telling her how much I enjoyed the way she was including students by having them act out scenes demonstrating various character traits they were studying. The more specific you are, the more meaningful the feedback.

Once I decided to provide a retiring teacher, Ginger Meyer, with a narrative of what it was like to watch her teach. I then shared it with the entire faculty for two reasons. First, it gave honor to her hard work and dedication to students. Second, it served as a model for ways everyone on our team can think about passionately serving students.

Here's an excerpt of the email I shared (with her permission):

> It's hard to describe what it's like to walk into a classroom when Ms. Meyer's students are singing. Thirty voices of blending notes, pitches, harmonies—such a stark contrast from the quiet hallway outside

her room. Students who may struggle in other settings flourish here; their faces lifted high and voices projecting with confidence.

And standing up front is Ms. Meyer, sleeves rolled up to her elbows, glasses perched on top of her head, lanyard of keys hung around her neck, and blond hair bouncing as she waves her hands. As her assistant Ms. Edens adds notes from the keyboard, Ms. Meyer dances in rhythm with the music and sings along.

Slowly, she is transforming a room full of students into a symphony of sound. She points, comments, and directs. She closes her eyes and is caught in the wave of voices—like a child riding a wave at the ocean; she seems to be floating higher with each note.

Or like a rider leading her horse into a canter or gallop, she opens the reins and prompts them into a full run. Now they are moving at full speed, sopranos hitting higher, altos blending, tenors and basses adding layers. And Ms. Meyer is over them all, her hair flying back as she feels the rumble, lifts the sound, and leads them higher and higher. She is soaring. She is transported.

And just as suddenly, she stops them all. "All right," she says, "We have three minutes. Watch your *e* vowels. Don't pinch off the notes." Like a coach to a team, she explains where they need to improve. And she makes them run the play again.

Divide and Delegate

Observing teachers, attending team meetings, attending games, and giving feedback require a lot of time, so rely on your team to help you. Not only can assistant administrators help, but other staff members may be able to help as well. For instance, my office secretary helps manage phone calls, maintenance requests, and substitute assignments so that I have more time for instructional leadership duties like classroom visits or supervision at activities. The more time you can devote to actually being in classrooms, with teams, or at school events, the better. These tasks cannot happen if you are flying solo. If you have teachers on your staff who can also provide strong instructional coaching, then also include them in ways they can be mentoring or assisting other teachers.

After one state track meet for our high school teams, I sent an email to our girls' track coach congratulating him and thanking him for his great photos and follow-up summaries he shares with our community. He replied with the following email:

> Just a sincere thank-you for supporting our kids. Not many student athletes have their athletic directors and especially principals at events very far from home. The kids notice, and their parents recognize the sincere effort taken by their child's school administrators. I know you were busy on Friday. I appreciate the effort of the entire building staff to help make the visit possible. (T. Wisely, personal communication, May 8, 2017)

What I appreciated about the email was that this coach recognized the part we all play in the message we send one another by being involved in supporting school activities, but also he knew my freedom to do so was the result of a strong school team of staff, teachers, and administrators who provide lots of support to make school successful when I am out of the building. Emails like this one are also good reminders that teachers understand the importance all our words and actions communicate to our school community.

Teachers are the most valuable resource schools have to promote student success. And even the most talented among them need and deserve meaningful feedback, coaching, and encouragement. To do this requires both formal and informal approaches—being visible throughout classrooms and activities, staying involved in team meetings, scheduling time with others in advance with flexibility, observing for understanding before giving written feedback, being specific with feedback and praise, maximizing face-to-face interaction, and relying on others to help with areas that may create more opportunities to be in classrooms or at events.

Now It's Your Turn

- What is one step you can take today to make your follow-up and messaging about instruction more meaningful for your teachers?
- How can you schedule your time in advance so that you do not miss out on valuable time in classrooms or at events?
- What is one digital tool you can begin using today to enhance the way you give feedback to others?

Apply Strategies for Facilitating Change

Britt Andreatta's (2017) book, *Wired to Resist*, explores the brain science behind why people are so naturally resistant to change. She discusses four stages our brains go through when confronted with change.

1. Shock and denial

2. Anger and fear

3. Acceptance and exploration

4. Commitment

I have found that educators follow these stages when it comes to new ideas, methods, or programs. Even good changes are stressful for most people. One of the mistakes school leaders often make in messaging with teachers is misunderstanding their need to plan for change. As school leaders, we may have great ideas on improvements, but we often fail to include our team in planning, developing, testing, and implementing changes far in advance. As a result of the problematic ways we manage change, teachers grow weary of being introduced to a new schedules or targets when they return to a new school year. What would happen if, instead, we began those conversations a semester or even a year before implementing something new?

In the fall semester of 2016, for example, we met with teacher teams and identified our need to redesign the way our schedule is built for remediating students. After we talked about options within our team meetings, we scheduled a professional development day for our entire faculty to look at goals for the second semester of the school year. Here was our guiding question: What actions, lessons, relationships, or decisions are we taking now that may affect next school year or years to come? As we continued the conversation we had been having about ways we can better influence students learning of essential skills, we decided to beta test some model schedules throughout the remaining spring semester, determine steps and tools for change, and then debrief to discuss feedback.

Use Beta Testing

What is beta testing? I read a blog post by educator A.J. Juliani (2016) titled "The Beginner's Guide to Design Thinking in the Classroom." Juliani is a firm believer that students learn best in scenarios that involve experiment and design. As I looked at the steps he suggests for building prototypes with students, I began asking, "How could this apply to schoolwide initiatives with teachers? If change is stressful, how can we practice change before it happens?" In other words, if my role as a school leader is to see my entire school as a macroversion of a classroom, how can I use these same design-thinking tips to affect our schoolwide planning and communication? Juliani's students often beta test ideas to see if they will work. So I asked, "Could beta testing change be a helpful strategy for teachers too?"

As my teachers and I realized our daily schedule was not structured well for supporting remediation pullouts, we commissioned a team including teachers, assistant principals, and a counselor to brainstorm ideas and draft some new trial schedules. This team came up with what they called GRIT schedules. GRIT would stand for *growth requires intense teamwork.*

After much planning, we had our first trial run with our new schedule right before a student holiday. Then, while students were on holiday, we met for a professional development day so that we could talk about the pros and cons of our first beta test.

Provide Steps and Tools for Change

Here's a breakdown of the four steps we took to prepare and test a first trial run on a proposed remediation schedule for an upcoming school year:

1. A team of teachers, administrators, and a counselor met weekly to look at models of remediation schedules and draft possible scenarios for our school.

2. This team created a mock daily schedule that we shared with faculty and students.

3. We shared a menu of sessions or classroom options with faculty and students.

4. We shared an Excel tracking sheet via so that teachers could preassign students to sections or classes for the remediation sessions. Other students could be targeted for study halls, tutoring, and so on.

Debrief Together for Feedback

As expected, the results of our first beta test were both positive and negative. In order to debrief, when we met as an entire faculty to review and to reflect on the trial run, we broke into seven groups and discussed the following questions.

1. For those involved in closed common formative assessment (CFA) classrooms, what were the positive outcomes?

2. For CFA classrooms, what improvements could be made for next time?

3. For those in open sessions, what were positive outcomes?

4. For open sessions, what improvements could we make for next time?

5. What were some unexpected challenges from GRIT time?

6. What are suggestions or ideas for making GRIT time more meaningful for all students?

Then we pulled back into one large group and allowed each group to report its feedback. The GRIT planning team took notes as they will continue meeting and developing more prototypes to test. In addition to teacher feedback, we also shared a SurveyMonkey with students so they can provide direct feedback as well.

After reviewing feedback from teachers and students, we re-evaluated and beta tested again. This time we chose a schedule slightly different from the first prototype. Yes, developing these plans, schedules, and resources required lots of work. But it was also a powerful lesson in collaboration and communication. The result? We settled on a plan for the next school year that will introduce a better remediation schedule so that our students have better, focused, collaborative supports for improved learning. And throughout the process, we communicated with teachers that growing together means implementing change together.

Yes, messaging includes the ways we publish, celebrate, and promote great learning moments within our schools. But it also involves the hard work of teamwork, planning, and collaboration with teachers. If you are going to see growth in learning and achievement, you must also be committed to communication strategies with teachers that include planning, beta testing, and problem solving together.

Now It's Your Turn

- What ways you are communicating with teachers on changes that need to take place for the next season of school?

- How do you anticipate resistance to change and implement processes for feedback and collaboration among teachers?

- What steps can you take to model or beta test ideas before full implementation of them?

Wrap Up

My wife and I have been married for almost twenty-four years at the time of this writing. When we were a young couple, I read a helpful book by Gary Chapman (1995) called *The Five Love Languages*. In it he explains the different ways each person likes to be appreciated: words of affirmation, acts of service, physical touch, time spent together, or active listening (Chapman, 1995). Chapman (1995) also explains that whenever you provide positive feedback to someone in the language they appreciate, you are making deposits in that person's love bank. When you provide negative feedback to someone, you are making withdrawals from his or her love bank. Over the years, I have learned that if my deposits outweigh my withdrawals, my marriage tends to positively reflect that investment. If, however, my withdrawals outnumber my deposits, it is time for some relationship intervention.

The same applies in all relationships. No matter how hard you work at messaging with teachers, you will inevitably fail to communicate an important item somewhere along the way. Accept that it is impossible to always communicate perfectly. But at the same time, commit to making deposits of positive communication that will outweigh the withdrawals of negative ones.

Your teachers are on the front lines of communicating with students, one another, and parents every day. If school leaders want to encourage great learning, our teachers need strong messaging from their leaders. Whether it is in classroom observations, face-to-face conversations, technology platforms, organized celebrations, or team building, your messaging with teachers matters. And the ability of your school to keep moving in the right direction will mirror the kind of commitment you are willing to make toward deep deposits in these important relationships.

Cultivating a Positive Message With Students

Seek first to understand, then to be understood.

—Stephen Covey

Cultivating a positive message with students is just as important for a leader as building positive messaging with teachers and staff. And messaging with students first begins like any other strong communication: trying to understand their perspective so that you can clearly understand their thoughts and needs.

Tim Elmore (2015), the founder of the organization Growing Leaders and author of books on emerging generations, researches the unique opportunities and challenges that our younger generations face in his book *Generation iY*. Generation iY students typically encompass those born sometime after 1990. They are the teens and college-age students who have never known a world without the Internet. Elmore (2015) also touches on the generation of students now stepping into the limelight: the *iGen* students who typically represent those born after the tragedies of September 11, 2001. This emerging generation has never known a world without global terrorism, economic uncertainty, or political unrest. Both the *Generation iY* and *iGen* students, however, have amazing opportunities and potential for making a difference in the world (Elmore, 2015).

Although their attention spans may be shorter than those of older generations, and their access to technology and information is unparalleled in history, students today are just as dependent on clear and concise information as any other generation. The tools may keep changing, but the messages must remain clear for students to thrive in school settings.

Consider the following scenario. Jenny is a returning eleventh-grade student at her high school. By the end of the summer, she's feeling more exhausted than relaxed. She hasn't picked up her fall schedule because she has been so busy with her summer job. She's overwhelmed knowing that the start of school means buying classroom supplies and paying fees that are hard for her to cover. Plus, she's wondering how she'll have the energy to work and do her schoolwork. She sets an alarm on her phone that wakes her up early enough for school, but she hits snooze and oversleeps. Her grandmother finally knocks on her door ten minutes before school starts.

When she arrives at school, she's missed breakfast and she's tardy. She stands in line at the counseling office to pick up her schedule. She glances over it and reads, "First hour, Mr. Samuels, room 125, Algebra 2." She doesn't recognize the teacher's name. She heads down the hall, flushed with frustration. She finds a seat still open in the back of the room. Then she slowly begins to realize that the teacher isn't talking about mathematics.

Jenny glances around the room but can't see the teacher's name anywhere. No one has a syllabus. Nothing is written on the board. She doesn't have any idea what room number this really is, but she has a feeling it's not room 125. By this time, she's too embarrassed to ask, and the teacher is so involved in his first-day-of-school speech that he hasn't paused to ask if anyone has questions. So Jenny endures the discomfort of being in the wrong class for the remaining forty-five minutes. Then she rushes out of the class before heading to the bathroom in tears.

Now let's meet Billy. Billy is a ninth grader who is starting a new school. When the big day comes, his father makes sure he wakes up early and is on time. He puts on new school clothes before devouring his favorite breakfast that his mother has made. He straps on his new backpack, making sure he has all his school supplies. Before he heads out the door, his mother takes his photo to post on Facebook.

Billy already has his schedule from the orientation meeting he attended the week before. When he walks into the school, he sees a table for students who requested schedule changes. He already has a schedule, so he finds another table in the cafeteria and waits. He notices the large television in the commons is scrolling welcome back messages with information about upcoming events. Soon the bell rings, and Billy heads to first hour.

His teacher is there to greet him at the door.

"Good morning," Mrs. Donovan says. "You'll find a seating chart on the SMART Board."

Billy looks at the screen and sees his name is listed on the fourth desk in the second row. When he sits down, he finds a folder with his name already written on it. When he opens it, he finds a class syllabus and calendar. There is also a half-page questionnaire for him to fill out. On the SMART Board above the seating chart, he reads, "You are in room 123, Mrs. Donovan's geography class, first period. Welcome!"

Billy sighs with relief. He is in the right place, and he knows what he should be doing because the leaders of his school have worked hard to cultivate positive messaging with students. This chapter discusses ways for leaders to cultivate such a message by ensuring a welcoming environment, celebrating student success, and appropriately communicating with students.

Ensure a Welcoming Environment

As you read both scenarios, you probably picked up on a few important observations in the strengths and weaknesses of each school's messaging and the different challenges facing both students.

Some students, like Billy, have a lot of support at home and at school. Billy doesn't have to worry about clothes or school supplies. He had a good breakfast. He's been to orientation. He has a schedule. He's prepared, and it makes the morning easier. Despite his good support at home, however, he still needs clear directions and guidance from school, which he gets, making his first day a smooth transition.

Jenny, on the other hand, is already struggling before she walks in the school doors from the overwhelming responsibilities she's managing outside of school. She's already working independently, and she doesn't seem to receive the kind of emotional and family support that would make school easier for her. Starting with inadequate support from home makes support at school even more important for her.

Billy's school environment and his teacher make it easy for him to feel secure and oriented. The school has anticipated student needs and developed a series of steps to give the students the information they need—from before they walk in the door to when they take their seats in the classroom. Billy thrives with the support he finds in his first moments at school and his first hour of class.

Jenny has made a big mistake going to the wrong class. Her school and teacher haven't provided any direction for students, exacerbating the problem. Her first-day experience was going to be tough enough because of her struggles outside of school; the additional lack of follow-through from her first-hour teacher (who isn't even her teacher) only adds to an already difficult situation. How different might her first day have been had she stepped into a school with a defined message like Billy's and then into a class like Mrs. Donovan's?

As you craft your communication plan for the school year, consider all the Billys and Jennys in your building. You can't control their experiences outside of school, but you play an enormous role in what kind of messages they receive in your school, and those messages begin on the very first days of school.

One of my favorite books to recommend to new teachers is Harry K. Wong and Rosemary T. Wong's (1998) *The First Days of School: How to Be an Effective Teacher*. In it, they outline the essentials for establishing, organizing, and implementing good routines and procedures for students. I call this skill teaching with both sides of your brain or teaching with one hand while managing with the other.

In a companion article, Wong and Wong (2000) remind teachers of seven questions students will have on the first day of school. These questions were first attributed to Douglas Brooks from the University of Texas-Arlington, who published an article on first days of school in 1985. Wong and Wong (2000) list the seven important questions Brooks discovered effective teachers anticipate.

1. **"Am I in the right room?"** Clearly mark locations and rooms throughout the school. Teachers help when they have their names clearly visible by the entrance or in the front of the room.

2. **"Where am I supposed to sit?"** Even high school students can benefit from assigned seating. It reduces anxiety and shows

students that teachers already know their names and have prepared for their arrival.

3. **"Who is the teacher as a person?"** Even though adults want to establish credibility and authority, they should also be approachable. Building a respectful rapport with students is key to engaging them in meaningful learning.

4. **"Will the teacher treat me as a human being?"** Remember your students are someone else's children. How we treat them is how we would want our own children treated: with patience, dignity, and compassion.

5. **"What are the rules in this classroom?"** School leaders and teachers should already know ahead of time what rewards and consequences are in store for students. Communicate these clearly, fairly, and consistently.

6. **"What will I be doing this year?"** Students are both global learners (needing the big picture) and sequential learners (requiring the steps for what to do next). It is important to address both styles of learning by giving students specific information on processes and upcoming schedules.

7. **"How will I be graded?"** Students need clear feedback on how teachers will measure their learning as well as how teachers will grade their work and how they can earn credits.

Indeed, learning to manage and instruct at the same time is key to an effective learning environment for all students. It is also essential if school leaders are to communicate expectations for an entire school.

Just as school leaders want teachers to clearly communicating expectations, these same reminders work throughout the entire school, and principals play an important role in modeling expectations and setting the tone for the entire school.

Figure 4.1 (page 66) is a checklist for the start of the school year that may help you as you frame the right messaging for your school.

Just like great teachers preemptively anticipate student needs, you can use those same skills, routines, expectations, and preparation to create messaging that builds a strong schoolwide climate from the very first days of school.

Start-of-School Checklist
- ☐ Do I use signs so new students know where they are and how to get to where they need to go?
- ☐ Are my hallways and buildings free from distracting clutter, creating an encouraging learning environment?
- ☐ Have I trained office staff on welcoming, greeting, and guiding guests who come to the school?
- ☐ Do we keep our calendar and website updated with current information?
- ☐ Have we printed student schedules in advance and made school maps available to students?
- ☐ Have we held an orientation meeting for incoming students and their parents?
- ☐ Have I published or emailed a welcoming, informative greeting to the school community?

Figure 4.1: Start-of-school checklist.

Visit go.SolutionTree.com/leadership to download a free reproducible version of this figure.

Now It's Your Turn

- Do you create a positive and supportive environment for students on the first day of school?
- How can you set the most positive tone possible for students entering your building and their classrooms?
- What ways can you prepare to immediately engage students in the learning process of school?

Once students have reached an understanding of the routines of the new school year, you can begin to attract raving fans by building momentum and harnessing the power of student engagement and enthusiasm to create a positive school culture students are excited about. As leader, you must embrace the role of being a chief communicator and cheerleader for your school community.

Celebrate Student Success

One way to harness enthusiasm and support positivity is to consistently celebrate all student success. Every day your students and their organizations achieve amazing results that leaders must make a point to celebrate, whether that's choir, band, Future Farmers of America, the debate team, the French club, the cross country team, or the National Honor Society. We begin the day by sharing these achievements through schoolwide morning announcements. Your school should also celebrate individual student learning accomplishments, such as what they do in particular classroom activities, like visuals or projects. We have a large television in our commons area that broadcasts announcements and photos of student achievement. We also email teachers copies of PowerPoint displays, slideshows, video clips, or photos so that they can display these on their SMART Boards in classrooms as ways for students to see other student achievement. Leaders and staff can share these accomplishments with the school community through emails, social media posts, and photos in local newspapers. Normally, teachers will email an announcement of celebration to me, and I will send it to our superintendent, our local newspaper editor, our school newsletter editor, and to our school's technology assistant who posts it on Facebook and Twitter. My recommendation is that something positive like this is being shared every day if not multiple times throughout the day. As we've increased the frequency of our social media posts, for example, more parents are engaging and leaving positive comments there as well.

Celebrating your students and school will look different from place to place. Whether you are in a large school, a small school, or at the elementary or secondary level, you still have wonderful, inspiring moments happening every day. Focus on these positives, and school becomes an exciting place to be.

For example, in my weekly newsletter, I regularly include six pages of color photos of our amazing students and teachers and their recent accomplishments. This digital newsletter is posted on our website as well as emailed to more than eight hundred parents and one hundred school employees throughout the community. Celebrations such as this contribute to the momentum necessary to keep a school moving in the right direction. People have a tendency to become sidetracked by negative or difficult moments, including school leaders. It is our job to confront problems and find solutions, but if the bulk of our communication with our students involves putting out fires then we have missed an important part of our role in consistently pointing them toward the goal of learning and growing. Complaints and challenges are inevitable, but with celebration, you have the power to overwhelm any negativity with the louder voice of positivity that comes through in your messaging. You have the ability to create raving fans.

Following are some examples of the approach for messaging we have implemented to engage students in the positive culture of our school so they become raving fans. Each year the student council decides on a motto for the school year. For example, one year student leaders researched the name of our school, Skiatook, which is a Native American name with uncertain etymology. What they discovered, however, is that our city is the only city called Skiatook in the world. So they came up with a two-part motto: "Don't forget to be awesome. And remember, there's only one Skiatook!" Mottos are like branding. As our students hear their class officers making daily announcements, they hear the same motto each day and are reminded that their school is a unique place with a lot of pride in its accomplishments. Our students elect class officers and student council officers each year who then collaborate on ideas for a new motto each school year.

Each morning starts with some expected routines that further support students' connection with the school as fans. Senior class officers participate in the morning announcements. Here is a sample script of one Friday morning announcement in the fall semester hosted by senior officers Jesse and Trace.

Jesse: Good morning Red Nation! It's game day and the rain won't stop our Bulldogs from busting out like a thunderstorm on the Buffaloes tonight.

Trace: Congratulations to the Future Farmers of America students who are showing livestock today at the Tulsa County Fair. And congrats to the cross country team for a great showing yesterday at Oklahoma Baptist University. Lily Cummings and Travis Hubbard placed in the top twenty and Jamie Ashford came in second place!

Jesse: Good luck to the Pride of Skiatook Band as they travel to compete tomorrow at the Ozarko Tournament in Springfield, Missouri.

Trace: Fall break begins Thursday, October 16. Due to the break, all Tulsa Community College and Tulsa Tech eligibility forms must be turned in to Ms. Goodell by Wednesday, October 15.

Jesse: Kudos to the volleyball and softball teams who both wrapped up their seasons this week. Thanks Lady Bulldogs for all the time and dedication you gave to your programs and to our school this fall season!

Trace: If you can't make it to tonight's game, follow all the Bulldog television action at Skiatook Bulldogs TV (http://skiatookbulldogs.tv). On the Bulldog TV website, you can also click the buttons to follow the game on Twitter or Facebook.

Jesse: Good luck tonight, Bulldogs! Have a fearless Friday. Don't forget to be awesome. And remember, there's only one Skiatook!

On this particular Friday, student leaders also prerecorded the announcement with music and saved it as an MP3 file so they could then email and feature it in multiple ways: audio, video, Facebook, Twitter, and the school website. (See chapter 5, page 81, for more ideas on using technology to feature students and their work.) When the school engages and acknowledges students in exciting ways, it creates momentum and brands the school as a place of excellence that values student contributions.

Sometimes the students themselves create the celebration. In these situations, school leaders can step in to support students. This is what happened in our school one year with Friday night football. One local television station holds a competition each week to see which schools are showing the most school spirit at Friday night games. Most weekends, the larger schools are showcased for their packed stadiums and excited fans. One year, however, a smaller school kept showing up on the news every Friday night: Skiatook! Why? The students began a grassroots campaign using Twitter to direct message the news reporters from the television station. They came up with different dress-up themes each week, and they inundated social media outlets with photos, videos, and updates of how they were dressing up and planning to be the most spirited fans at upcoming games. Their eagerness was so contagious that parents began to participate as well. One evening, students organized a stadium event that had every adult attendee joining the students in throwing baby powder into the air during a stadium cheer sung in unison. It looked like a huge cloud of smoke had erupted from the entire stadium, and the television stations were there to capture it. At the end of the school year, a Tulsa station awards a trophy to one school as fans of the year. All the big schools were finalists, but one smaller school, Skiatook, won the award. *Don't forget to be awesome. And remember, there's only one Skiatook.*

It is easy to dismiss the enthusiasm and fervor of students and sports teams as random, unexpected moments; however, I believe that the momentum of positivity from a variety of events grows with time throughout your entire school culture.

Once a teacher at my school told me she was having a bad day. Some of her students had been challenging, and she was having a hard time keeping a positive outlook. After classes that day, she visited the girls bathroom. She was surprised to see someone had a left a sticky note on the mirror that said, "You are enough." Another note said, "You are loved." Suddenly, she felt better and smiled at the kind sentiments.

There on the soap dispenser sat a notepad of sticky notes and a pen. A note on front of the dispenser said, "Take a sticky note and add your own!" Underneath it read another note saying, "I just want to let whoever did this know you are an amazing person, the world needs more people like you!" These were all written with student handwriting. And so throughout the day, girls added more notes: "We want the very best for you!" and on and on. Before long some teachers decided to expand the display. They hung a sheet of butcher paper on the wall with the inscription, "Take what you need! Give what you can!"

Underneath sat a small table with notepads, pens, and lotion. More messages were added, and soon a rainbow of florescent pinks, yellows, greens, and blues dotted the background: "You are beautiful for you are fearfully and wonderfully made." "Good News: Nothing Lasts Forever. Push On!" "Don't let negative things get to you." "Love yourself!"

A few days later, we began to share photos of these moments on Facebook, Twitter, and via email. That same day, I received a phone call from a local reporter, Ryan Braschler, who wanted to do a story on the bathroom. He arrived right at the end of the school day and published the story for that evening's news. (Visit http://ktul.com/news/local/the

-writing-on-the-wall-in-skiatook-hs-girls-bathroom to watch the news story on the bathroom.)

It was so exciting to see the momentum building as people from inside and outside our community celebrated these little acts of kindness. I don't believe these acts are an accident or isolated incidents. Rather, they are evidence of our student council's campaign called the Class Cup Challenge. Throughout the semester, teachers submit student names for good deeds they have observed. For instance, one teacher gave kudos to a boy who went out of his way to pick up someone else's trash left on a table after breakfast. Another student was tagged for helping tutor another student. As this practice became contagious, our student council members met and made award certificates for good deed recipients. They deliver the certificates during classes so students are acknowledged in front of their peers. At the end of the year, the class with the highest total points is awarded a Class Cup trophy.

I am not saying there is a direct correlation between school branding and success in student activities or learning. At the same time, when school leaders welcome student involvement, encourage creative displays of school branding, and invite student participation through social media, the entire environment of the school becomes electric with excitement. School culture can cultivate creativity, enthusiasm, and celebration around student success. And subsequently, success tends to breed success.

Now It's Your Turn

- What is a theme or motto your school can rally around to build excitement?
- What are routines or rituals you can use to motivate student enthusiasm?
- What is one step you can take to provide a stronger platform for celebrating student achievement?
- In what ways do your students already drive celebration in your school?

Communicate With Students

I once knew a student who struggled with many issues due to her home environment. She didn't always make the best decisions, even though after a lot of intervention, she was finally passing all of her classes. One day, I met with her after she had skipped school, and I assigned her to our in-school placement room (one teacher and no social interaction for the day) for discipline. When she caught up on her work, she sent a note to my office asking if she could read something. I looked over the books in my office and chose a copy of *Chicken Soup for the Teenage Soul* for her. A few hours later, she sent another note asking if she could see me. When she came into my office, she told me that she had read the entire book and wanted another. I was surprised, so I quizzed her on different chapters of the book. Sure enough, she had read it all, and she told me this was one of the first books she had ever read that told stories that reminded her of her own life. I picked up my office phone and called our school librarian who sent over a copy of *Chicken Soup for the Woman's Soul*. My student asked if she could take it home. When I told her the librarian said she could have it for two weeks, she clutched it to her chest and beamed.

"Awesome!" she shouted.

You would have thought it was a Christmas present. I'll never forget the look of delight and joy on her face, and I remember when she left my office, I thought back over my day. I had a lot of challenges, but that one moment made every challenge worth it (Parker, 2014). The magic of that moment, however, did not just happen because of that one day. Being able to communicate deeply about the student's interests, holding her accountable to expectations, and encouraging her toward new ideas came after months of tough conversations and consistent interventions.

As you work to create strong messaging in your school, you must also keep in mind how to effectively communicate with and reach all students—including those who present challenging behaviors. With that in mind, here are seven ways to keep your messaging strong with students.

Communicate Dignity and Respect

It is worth remembering that all students respond more positively when they feel that they are valued and significant. Raymond J. McNulty and Russell J. Quaglia (2007) explore the work of the International Center of Leadership Excellence, and how their work with model schools shows three components—rigor, relevance, and relationship—are necessary for student achievement. When it comes to the effects of positive teacher and student rapport, McNulty and Quaglia (2007) state:

> Relationships do not become a new standard or replace rigor and relevance. They are a way to improve learning. The recent work of the International Center has examined some of the most successful high schools in the country—schools that have the challenges of poverty, mobility, and diversity but still have high rates of student success.
>
> In these schools, relationships among students and staff are deliberately nurtured and a key reason for student success. Students believe the staff genuinely cares about them and encourages them to achieve at high levels. If there is not a high level of positive relationships, students will not respond to higher expectations.

As a classroom teacher, I started my career in a large district near Tulsa, Oklahoma. My students represented a mixture of demographics and backgrounds. Every day I would begin my classes by saying, "I am glad you are here today." Inevitably, a student would ask, "Why do you say that each day?" I would explain, "Because you could choose to be anywhere else. You don't have to follow the law, obey your parents, or stay in school if you choose otherwise. But you have chosen to be here today, and I am glad you did."

Treating others with dignity doesn't mean being a pushover, but it does mean finding a way to show students that you value them—so when the time comes for you to offer correction or assign discipline, students know you care about them. At the schoolwide level, leaders communicate these values with the way they address students, the tone of voice they use, and the words they choose to say. Students can sense whether leaders have their best interests in mind. Whether you are making announcements, communicating directions, or celebrating successes, make it a goal to speak to your students in ways that show you respect and value them. A colleague of mine once taught in a school where an administrator would make schoolwide intercom announcements lecturing students for being tardy to class. As a teacher, she always cringed at the harsh tone as well as the ineffective strategy for modifying student behavior. If, on the other hand, school leaders enforce consistent follow-through on student discipline for students who are chronically late to class as well as highlight and celebrate those who are responsible and on time, then you set a tone of respect and positive expectations for student behavior.

Keep Your Messages Positive

As you establish connections, routines, instructional practices, and so on, stay focused on the tasks at hand, and speak to the positive behaviors you expect from students rather than overcommunicating about the negative ones you want to correct. For instance, the leadership team of administrators and counselors at our high school begins every school year by meeting with students in classrooms. We choose small settings to talk about handbooks and expectations for the school year. Yes, we touch on the rules and policies, but we also talk about what goals we want each student to set for his or her years in high school. Although I know some students are more likely to advance or excel than others based on their past records, I talk to all of them with the expectation that they want to perform at the highest levels.

One analogy I use with students is a soccer game. Imagine you show up to a soccer game. Each team is on the field. Parents and fans are present to cheer. Referees are in place to officiate. The head referee blows the whistle to start the game. Suddenly, you look down the field and realize there is no goal for the goalie to guard. In fact, there are no goals at either end of the field. The referee blows the whistle to stop the game, and everyone is confused. Then I ask students, "What do you think the game would look like if they decided to keep playing without goals? The players would look silly; they would be all dressed up and running plays but never able to score or reach their goal. That is what school looks like when you just show up with no specific learning goals in mind." We try to paint a picture for them of what the coming school year will look like, the disciplines they should practice for learning, and how to reach their goals of growing, earning good grades, and gaining new knowledge.

Even as you build positive expectations, it's inevitable that some students will still make bad choices. Don't let these negative behaviors define your school's message. Don't allow yourself to let isolated instances of challenging behavior turn into public discussions that may not be necessary for everyone to hear. For example, if you have a high school student who is parking illegally, identify him or her and correct the behavior. Don't waste the power of your messaging by making announcements to everyone in the school about parking rules when only a handful of students may need the correction. This doesn't mean you don't express disappointment or correct misbehavior, but do so in a way that addresses the behavior of those involved while avoiding statements that are unnecessary to everyone at large. As you apply this rule of thumb throughout your school, you allow the positive behaviors to define what is normal in the climate of your school.

Be Consistent

Sometimes you will face the temptation to escalate a challenging moment by fighting fire with fire. In the heat of the moment, it is easy to lose control of your words and emotions. Usually, these moments will just create more combustion. In your messaging with challenging students in mind, focus on the purpose at hand. If you have specific goals for your school, then stay focused on those goals. All students thrive when they know what to expect, so stay consistent in the way you handle interactions, consequences, and follow-through. It is also important for some messaging to be predictable and routine. Some elementary schools, for instance, have daily or weekly school assemblies to sing together, praise success, and recite school creeds. High school students also thrive on routine. At my son's elementary school, Hayward Smith Elementary, in Owasso, Oklahoma, Principal Pat James and his teachers begin each Monday morning in the gym with students before school. During that time, they sing the school song together, recognize student birthdays with songs and dancing, and recognize student achievement with awards. They remind students to practice good behavior and show strong character. The atmosphere is encouraging and positive. Don't be afraid to include fun activities, music, or visuals in communication with secondary students too. These kinds of rituals go a long way in consistent practices of sharing the positive messages you want all students to remember each of day of school. You will still correct individual behavior when you need to, but your school community gets a consistent diet of positive messages.

Be Human

Students often relate to you better when they see you as a person, not just an educator. Again this does not mean sacrificing your dignity, but it might mean taking risks to communicate authentically. When I was in the classroom, for instance, I would bring my guitar to school and sing to my high school students. We would learn silly rhymes together for remembering grammar rules. These teaching strategies always required me to step out of my comfort zone. But students were more likely to engage and learn when I was willing to take risks. As a principal, I have played piano for students when they sing for senior assemblies. Both students and parents have expressed to me afterwards that they appreciate seeing me in a way that is unexpected or surprising to them. One year as a classroom teacher, for instance, I decided to use a common personal theme in grammar and punctuation practices. To hook my students, I included references to my favorite dessert: frozen custard. As I created sample sentences for my students to correct, for instance, I would find ways to work in how much I love frozen custard. My students thought it was silly, but they paid attention and learned. I didn't realize I was also drumming up lots of business for the nearest frozen custard shop. Our local custard shop saw so much business from my students that they began giving me free frozen custard treats for sending them customers! Allow yourself, your teachers, and your staff to express their individuality in ways that entertain and inspire learning. When you do, your students relate to you in ways that help them connect to the message you're delivering.

Be Professional

Professionals are experts in their areas, strong in customer service, and committed to improved outcomes. No matter how much you try to connect with students, you are always an educator, so as you work to improve your messaging with all students, be sure your communication is always professional and establishes trust. Students should not be privy to confidential information or conflicts among school staff. Even as you communicate with challenging students, address them with firmness, fairness, and consequences while staying focused on the goal of helping them make the right decisions. By all means, be the adult in the way you communicate, and don't allow conflict to derail the power of your message.

Provide Resources and Support

In *A Framework for Understanding Poverty*, Ruby K. Payne (2005) explains eight resources every student needs to be successful.

1. Financial resources

2. Emotional resources

3. Mental ability and acquired skills

4. Spiritual guidance or purpose

5. Physical health and mobility

6. Support systems, such as friends, family, and available backup resources

7. Relationships and role models

8. Knowledge of hidden rules or knowing unspoken cues and habits of a group

At-risk students such as Jenny typically lack one or more of these essential supports. Students who thrive typically have all eight. Positive and effective communication won't help students if you fail to address their most basic needs; otherwise, messaging about your school is little more than propaganda. So be an advocate for students to find the resources they need.

In our community, a group of retired teachers and area ministers formed a nonprofit organization that helps families in need. The organization is called Skiatook Emergency Action Committee (SEAC), and it provides thousands of dollars of charitable donations in the form of food items, clothing, or help with utilities. Our district employees can opt to have money automatically deducted from their paychecks to donate to SEAC each month. When the school becomes aware of students in need, SEAC intervenes. For instance, one student lost his home in a fire, and SEAC immediately responded with donations, gift cards, and groceries. Every school should have a comprehensive approach to understanding the various needs of students so that supports are in place to meet their needs. When your school is a place of learning that also addresses student needs, then you have a strong environment worth celebrating. In other words, messaging cannot simply exist in a vacuum. You must use it in the context of surrounding students with the services and resources that address their needs to be successful in school.

When educators commit to sharing common values and practices for addressing the financial, emotional, mental, physical, relational, and cultural needs of students, they have healthy soil for cultivating a strong learning environment.

Stay Hopeful Even While Accepting the Outcome

You have to accept that even with your best efforts in messaging or caring, you cannot control all outcomes. This is difficult for a lot of educators to accept; however, it should also be reassuring to know that you have done your best. One student we worked with over a four-year period during high school was eventually placed in an inpatient facility for drug rehabilitation after many failed attempts on our part to help him. His school counselor and I would often celebrate a move forward, only to grieve when he took several steps backward. He eventually found a successful path to finishing school and a good career in the military. Not all stories have a happy ending, though. As you work with students, sometimes you will encounter profound disappointment. All of these ups and downs are a normal part of education, so keep them in perspective, communicate your expectations, celebrate wins, and accept the reality that there are still outcomes you can't completely control.

When I was growing up in a small, rural community in West Tennessee, I didn't know what Title I benefits were and that I qualified for them. I didn't realize that the students getting the benefits of free lunches and a reading remediation tutor were classified as in need or at risk. I just knew that my parents and teachers believed in me. I really thought I could do anything if I set my mind to it. When I became a teacher, I began to realize the value of educators who had believed in me, held me accountable, and challenged me. I would never have learned without their amazing support; they even gave me that support at the times when I didn't deserve it. No matter how much progress you make in messaging with students, you will have days in which difficulties are inevitable and students disappoint you. When that happens, stay consistent and firm. Deal with the defiance or disappointment with appropriate consequences or discipline. Accept setbacks and move on. Keep investing in all students, and keep finding ways to communicate those wins to a larger audience. Provide students with consistency— no matter how challenging their behaviors might be—without being diverted from setting strong goals, communicating those goals, and reaching them.

Now It's Your Turn

- In what ways can you organize messaging to stay consistent, no matter how challenging some of your days may be?

- What are some rituals, routines, or practices you can be using to create expectations for a strong learning environment?

- What ways are you willing to take risks in connecting with students so that they can better relate to your direction, instruction, or leadership?

- What resources can you identify to help students so that they can be successful learners?

Wrap Up

For most of my school years, I attended a local K–8 school. When I started high school, my father re-enlisted in the Navy, and we lived in three different states during those years: Tennessee, New York, and Virginia. Being a new student in three different high schools was overwhelming and scary. As a career educator, I have served in four different schools. As someone who has consistently experienced what it is like to be new to a school, I have a lot of empathy for students who are new. At the same time, the longer I am invested in the to-dos of a school, the harder it becomes to take a step back and look at my school school from the perspective of a new student. But I believe it is a healthy practice to constantly look at your school with fresh eyes. From the visual cues like signage to the kinds of announcements that are made, how do we create the kind of learning environment with our messaging that provides students a sense of stability, expectation, and confidence in their school? Messaging with the perspective of the student in mind means a constant commitment to how you communicate throughout your entire school year. The good news is that we can always keep growing in the ways we target communication with students. And, as technology grows, we also have more tools available to us than ever before for amplifying those messages.

Using Technology to Message With Students

If you don't give people information, they'll make something up to fill the void.

—Carla O'Dell

As you think through the ways to build and communicate a culture of engagement and enthusiasm among students in your school, you will likely realize that some of the best ways to do this are with digital tools. The technology strategies I highlight in this chapter will point you in the right direction as you start building your school's messaging with students. Although changes in technology are swift, the tools, programs, and applications that follow illustrate the powerful ways you can use technology to build a positive school culture. Remember that methods may change, but positive messages are worth sharing, no matter what technology next emerges.

This chapter explores how to best employ specific technology tools in your messaging with students and how to create and implement weekly student newsletters.

Employ Technology Tools

There are so many different ways you can connect with students via technology: Twitter, Facebook, and Instagram, to name a few. Elmore (2015) shares that among youth, "6 percent watch Netflix, 75 percent post on Facebook, 73 percent shop online, 49 percent Tweet, 43 percent read an e-book." He also quotes a Kaiser Family Foundation Report that found "in February 2010 . . . kids between eight and eighteen are spending seven-and-a-half hours each day in front of a screen," and a Nielsen Company survey (Elmore, 2015) reports that the "typical U.S. teen mobile subscriber sends or receives an average of 1,742 texts per month" (pp. 27–28).

Use Social Media

Find a few social media tools that work best for you and stick to regular, scheduled communication via those outlets. For instance, at our high school we have designated one staff person, a technology assistant, who monitors and posts our Facebook, Twitter, and Instagram pages. Our strategy is as follows: when teachers, staff, or administrative team members report learning or celebration moments, they email a summary and photos to our entire high school teacher list. Also, each student in our school is given a school email address. Students from clubs, activities, or sports can also email photos or reports to the technology assistant or me. Our technology assistant then takes content or photos and reposts them on the school's Facebook, Twitter, and Instagram pages. The benefit of having one person manage the postings is that she can control content as well as monitor comments or edit posts. Our counseling office keeps a list of any students whose parents have requested their child's photos not be shared publicly. Normally, that list includes only a few names, as most parents love to see postings of their children from school. When students or parents see the postings, they can leave comments. Since our high school sites are public pages, most of the interactions on it are positive, and our technology assistant keeps a close eye on our pages. One tool she uses to create or schedule posts is a website called Hootsuite (https://hootsuite.com). Hootsuite allows you to create a dashboard of all your social media outlets, including Facebook, Twitter, Instagram, LinkedIn, or Pinterest. You can draft one post on Hootsuite with photos or links and then schedule it be posted on all other social media platforms at the same time. The Hootsuite dashboard allows you to see all your social media feeds on one page, which is helpful if you use multiple social media platforms.

Create Promotions

Look for technology tools that allow you to showcase your students and their accomplishments. Educators may not have formal training in marketing and design, but tools like PowToons (www.powtoon.com), a free program to create animated videos and presentations, and Biteable (https://biteable.com), a free video maker, provide easy ways to promote the positive message of your school to students.

Visit the website for Skiatook High School (www.skiatookschools.org/schools/skiatook-high-school) to see a short video montage titled "Excellence Enters Here" created using PowToons. In the PowToons video clip we created, animated fingers scroll words across the screen that say "Welcome to Skiatook High School. Your Place to Excel. School Pride. Perseverance. Leadership. Learning. Growing. Excellence Enters Here." Each subtitle has a background photo of students in action. Music plays along in the background, and the overall image is one that highlights the best moments of our school. You can connect with students by playing such videos during events. We played our PowToons video to a group of two hundred incoming ninth graders. To my surprise, when they video finished, they broke into applause.

Our student council leadership students have also learned the power of creating promotions using Biteable. When they announced the new Class Cup initiative, they created a video to show at a student assembly. The video explained with words, graphics, and music how each grade could earn points throughout the school year by participating in spirit events, good behavior, and demonstrating good deeds.

Feature Announcements

One simple way you can enhance communication with your students is by sharing daily announcements in easy-to-use formats like PowerPoint. So in addition to reading announcements every morning, you can also feature them throughout the school during the entire school day. This way, students have a visual reminder of important events and other announcements in classrooms on SMART Boards and in places like the cafeteria area. Our high school commons area has a large flat-screen television mounted on the wall so students can see announcements displayed throughout the day. Begin the year by creating an announcement template in PowerPoint, and then assign a staff member or student to update them daily. You can also email the slideshow file to teachers and staff. As we share announcements, our technology assistant also reposts important information on our social media platforms and website.

Announcements don't have to be visual only—you can also feature recorded announcements using technology tools such as GarageBand (www.apple.com/mac/garageband; Apple only). PC users can use LMMS, a free open-source software download for recording voice or audio (https://lmms.io). During football season, students enjoy jazzing up the morning announcements with prerecorded audio announcements. By adding an audio clip of our school fight song, our student officers will record an intro that sounds more like a radio show than a school announcement. We play these clips on Friday to celebrate game day, and they are always a favorite of students and teachers. We also embed other school announcements of upcoming events or congratulations to other student activities with these same audio recordings. Visit the Skiatook Public Schools (n.d.a.) website goo.gl/uSXWXV to hear an example of the announcements created using GarageBand. I also use GarageBand to record podcast episodes. If you want to hear a sample, check out this episode in which I interview our student council leadership students on their involvement in promoting a movement of kindness: goo.gl/Vmvyty.

Post Movies

Use tools such as Windows Movie Maker or iMovie to create movies that celebrate school victories or highlight student achievements. Both tools are easy to use to create clips with video and audio components and then post them on a video-sharing service like YouTube. I often record student voices to feature on the movies using GarageBand. Another way I have shared posts is via YouTube. For instance, one day I used my iPhone to record video of our band rehearsing before school, students in each class period of the day, students going to classes through the hall, lunchtime in the school commons area, and afternoon sports activities. I put these all together in a sixty-second video called *1 Day in 1 Minute* to share with students, teachers, and the community so that others could have a glimpse of school life around the entire campus.

Use Reminder Applications

Many educators have discovered the convenience of reminding students and parents of upcoming events with text-based application subscription tools such as Remind (www.remind.com). These are simple to use and safe for one-way communication. Remind has also created options for chatting between users, so some back-and-forth conversation can happen as well without having to text or email. Some of our high school juniors and seniors can enroll in concurrent classes off campus through career technology or community colleges. We set up a Remind account for currently enrolled students so they have weekly reminders from the school that we couldn't deliver to them otherwise since concurrent students are off campus half the day.

It will not take long for some of these tools to become obsolete, but the goal is to continually identify ways students in your community can effectively receive good news about what's happening in your school.

Now It's Your Turn

- What is one new tool you can commit to using over the next thirty days to enhance your student outreach?

- What is one way you are already consistently communicating with students? How could you enhance those messages with technologies that students are already using?

- Who is someone on your team you could designate for helping with technology support?

Release Weekly Student Newsletters

A weekly student newsletter is another option for featuring student achievement and school successes as well as connecting with students on a regular basis. There are many options for newsletters—from a simple text format to a colorful, information-packed update on student and classroom achievements. In the past, we mailed home copies of our newsletter. Now our newsletter has become digital only, and over eight hundred parents subscribe to receive it via email. Following are seven steps to implement this effective communication tool with your students.

1. Collect and build content.

2. Organize information into categories.

3. Assign student roles.

4. Create your draft template.

5. Proof and review.

6. Share digitally.

7. Don't let mistakes stop the momentum.

The following sections explain each of these steps in more detail.

Collect and Build Content

Throughout the week, collect ideas, stories, photos, web addresses, and information about students, teachers, and events—anything positive that has been happening at school. For instance, if a student was recognized in the local news for an award or activity, copy that link to include in your newsletter postings as well. Or if a teacher has a classroom or club Facebook page, include a link to the original post. Staff members can email this type of information about their classes, teams, or groups directly to their teacher leaders who can then store them in a digital folder you create. I use a Google setting that tags any online news story that mentions "Skiatook High School," then automatically emails these stories to me so that I can be one of the first to see any information being published about my school in other media sources and potentially include them in the newsletter. You can create as many alerts as you would like by visiting www.google.com/alerts and enter the words or phrases you want to tag. Google will automatically email you alerts on those word or phrase choices as stories appear in the news or online about them.

Here's a list of content ideas you could use for a newsletter.

- Innovative lessons or projects from classroom activities

- Award winners in clubs, activities, or sports

- Updates on recent events, assemblies, or competitions

- Announcements of upcoming events

- Reminders of how to check grades or attend tutoring

- Students of the month

- Teachers of the month
- Calendar updates
- Fund-raiser announcements or other deadlines, like ordering yearbooks

Organize Information Into Categories

Our newsletter is a combined effort. I have a newsletter teacher who keeps an Edmodo (www.edmodo.com) file where he stores any emails or announcements being shared via email or social media about student achievement. Edmodo is an online digital hub where teachers can post assignments or have discussions with students about digital projects. He shares the latest information for his students to access, and they help create upcoming newsletter publications. As various items, photos, and messages come in, he collects them in this central location for easy access. If you have a publishing class, have students keep a running list of items they plan to edit, draft, and post for publishing by the end of each week.

Assign Student Roles

Teachers and even parents can be great resources for photos or information on student achievement; however, students can also be reporters, photographers, editors, and image editors. In our newsletter class, each student researches different topics, including athletics, academics, activities, the school calendar, student life, scholarships, counseling, lunch menus, big events, student achievements, teacher achievements, and so on. A staff member always needs to review and edit student articles before publishing, but the main goal is consistent collection of news on student and school successes. Teachers and school leaders also write summaries of student achievements and submit photos to include. Unlike a traditional school newspaper, a school newsletter is more of a compilation of all the great events, news, announcements, or celebrations happening on a weekly basis throughout the school.

Create Your Draft Template

Students collect, create, and share content through Edmodo so they can access documents by one another and their teacher at any time. Specific students transfer the content to Microsoft Publisher, adding headings, photos, and so on. Throughout the week, students work collaboratively to edit and expand the draft. Keeping a consistent format helps promote your school's logos, images, and branding. Figure 5.1 is a sample of how we format our newsletter.

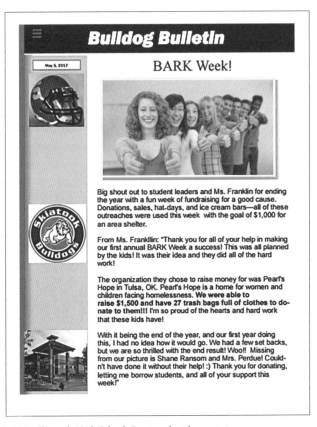

Source: © 2017 Skiatook High School. Reprinted with permission.

Figure 5.1: *Bulldog Bulletin.*

Tasks can rotate to involve all students. For instance, on Mondays and Tuesdays, students write, create, and build content into their template. By Wednesday, they are getting to their final edits. Not every schedule will look the same for each school, so find a plan that works for you. The key is to set consistent routines if you want to create a publication each week to share from your school.

Proof and Review

Once the document is complete, a trusted adult should review the final proofs, save the publication as a PDF, and link the file to the school website. We review drafts twice. First, a desktop publishing teacher reviews the draft copy. Then, I review and edit the final copy. If this is not a strength area for you, find someone in your school who enjoys proofing to partner with students.

Even as you publish one newsletter, your student team begins immediately on content for the next week's publication. This may be the hardest part of consistent communication, but you will find that the gathering and sharing of news really never stops.

Share Digitally

Compose an email via whatever system you use for bulk emailing and link to the student newsletter. I suggest you also post a link on your school website. Whatever format is best for your school, share often so that everyone has easy access to student news. We also share a link to the newsletter via social media platforms so students or parents can see the content on phones or other devices by following an embedded link back to the newsletter. Occasionally, we print copies of the newsletter to share with local organizations like the Rotary Club or Chamber of Commerce, but mostly we keep the content available on our website.

Don't Let Mistakes Stop the Momentum

When publishing frequent, consistent messages, you will also find that sometimes errors or mistakes occur. As important as it is to set a good example in grammar, punctuation, and content, do not allow these mishaps to keep you from creating and publishing the next newsletter.

Involving students and teachers in your weekly newsletter publications can be hard work. But it is worth it when it expands the way you communicate about your school. When you use the best resources for communication—your students—you enhance your ability and theirs to promote positive messages about your school's successes. To view examples of our student newsletter, *Bulldog Bulletin*, visit the Skiatook Public Schools (n.d.b.) website (http://bit.ly/2vovffV) to find archived copies.

- How do you currently share student and school news in a consistent way? Do you involve students in this sharing?

- Who in your school or organization has the skills and student connections to take your publications to the next level?

- Is there an easier format for you than a traditional newsletter? Perhaps you would be more comfortable with a weekly photo or video share. Whatever means you choose, keep sharing the positive messages from your school!

Wrap Up

If you are a school leader who is *not* using technology to consistently communicate messages to your school community, you are not being heard. You may as well be leading from another planet with no connections back to your counterparts on planet Earth. Without the use of technology, no one is aware of your school's hard work, contributions, or successes.

While that might seem like an exaggeration, the point I'm trying to make is that school leaders can no longer enjoy the luxury of expecting someone else to figure out how to use technology to communicate school messages. Yes, leaders need talented and gifted team members who are technology experts; however, the use of technology is now essential to leadership practices. Over the years, I have had to learn to become comfortable with the idea that some of my teachers pay more attention to text messages than email. I have had to learn that just because a news item is placed on a marquee or a website does not mean any students or parents have actually seen the message.

We must constantly be seeking relevant ways for connecting messages back to people in the various ways they will best hear them or see them. Learning to use technology to create messages for students and your school community means embracing old tools and new tools. It means being comfortable that the options are ever changing. It means accepting the reality that one message must be communicated in as many ways as possible for the most exposure.

The good news is that as you commit to being a student of new tools and technologies, you become a model for others, and your teachers and students can accelerate and amplify your efforts. One summer I used Biteable for the first time to create a welcome-back-to-school promotional video. Once my teachers and students saw it, they began to create their own videos for classrooms and assemblies. One teacher created a *welcome to my class* video using Biteable. Our student leadership team created a Class Cup Challenge video using Biteable. Their productions were much better than my original, and that makes me happy.

I believe the biggest challenge for leaders with technology is the overwhelming number of choices. Keep it simple. Focus on just one new technology to use for messaging. What is an upcoming letter to parents or announcement to students you need to share? How would you normally share that information? Now, ask yourself, "What is one new technology I haven't used before that I can use to also share this information?" Ask students or teachers for help. Once you have figured out that new tool, place it in your arsenal of options. And then choose another to learn. Don't let yourself off the hook when it comes to staying up to date or relevant when it comes to messaging. Yes, using technologies to enhance messaging takes time. The alternative, however, is remaining silent to a community that needs to hear your voice reminding them of the purposes, goals, and achievements you are experiencing together.

6

Cultivating a Positive Message With Parents and the Community

I'm a great believer that any tool that enhances communication has profound effects in terms of how people can learn from each other, and how they can achieve the kind of freedoms that they're interested in.

—Bill Gates

I have a secret to share with you. Actually, you probably already know it: at night, when students talk to their parents about their day, they talk about their teachers. And they talk about their principal as well. Sometimes they share the funny, engaging, or inspiring moments from their school day. At other times, they share their embarrassing or upsetting moments that adults may have mismanaged—or even caused. Parents and the community learn about your school, in part, from the experiences students share. Indeed, your school is more than just a place of learning; it is an experience. Given this, you might say that educators and school leaders are involved in public relations every day that they work in school.

As educators, it is easy to forget how the community—both local and worldwide—perceives our schools. Lessons from public relations, marketing, and customer service can help improve climate and how others perceive schools. This chapter discusses how to make public relations a priority, how to build a platform for communicating, and how to partner with parents.

Make Public Relations a Priority

One summer, our school district leadership team sat down with a public relations consultant, Jeremy C. Burton, who has managed public relations for two Oklahoma universities. The school he was serving at the time had seen an upward surge in enrollment and development. A focus on public relations played an important role in promoting its brands and messages (Risseghem, 2009). Burton shared four insights for employing dynamic communication that also apply to K–12 schools (J. Burton, personal communication, June 10, 2015).

1. Make solid decisions—they are the bedrock of good public relations.

2. Give context to difficult decisions.

3. Communicate with honor.

4. Embrace social media.

Make Solid Decisions

You can never underestimate the potency of bad decisions. No matter the size of your school community or the amount of resources you can dedicate to public relations, every positive message you send begins with the decisions you make on a daily basis. One positive example of this at Skiatook came during a high school graduation ceremony. We discovered that a former student, a World War II veteran, had never received his high school diploma. So we invited him to attend our graduation ceremony to finally honor him with a graduation certificate. A family member reached out to local television and newspaper outlets, and they covered the story. For days following the ceremony, I received kind notes and emails from people thanking us for paying tribute to a deserving veteran. The good decision on the part of our district to give honor where it was due brought the district honor in the process.

Not every decision has been such a good one, unfortunately. Several years ago, we failed to alert students to an important event. At the start of October, high school juniors interested in scholarships to college are able to take the Preliminary SAT/National Merit Scholarship Qualifying Test—the PSAT. This is the only time a high school student can test to qualify for this potentially prestigious recognition. We assumed this was common knowledge and did not include the test dates anywhere in our publications for parents. Later in the year, a parent shared his disappointment that his student missed out on the opportunity to take the test. This feedback was helpful in so many ways. It was a pivotal conversation for me in that it helped me begin a new journey of learning better ways to message with parents. Also, it gave me perspective on how easy it is for students and parents to miss out on important opportunities. Since then, we have made it a priority to overcommunicate dates and deadlines.

Give Context to Difficult Decisions

When you are making a tough decision, give the reasons for the decision in a clear and empathetic way. It's helpful to think of the moon example from earlier in this book. No matter how much you look at the moon, you can only see the side visible to the Earth. You may understand the reasons behind a complicated decision, but others may not be privy to the details surrounding your choice. When it is possible to share the context, however, you build stronger consensus. For example, when our school district passed its last bond issue, our superintendent held multiple community meetings to seek input from employees, patrons, and parents on priorities for upcoming growth. The board then shared final decisions—decisions that allowed community buy-in and support long before the school board voted to bring the bond issue to a vote of the community.

Communicate With Honor

What tone do you appreciate when others communicate with you? Most of us appreciate when we're treated with dignity and respect. Leaders must consider that their words, tone, and attitude influence their message. For instance, during a school crisis or emergency, it is important for every staff member to know his or her role and what steps to take next. Our school district is in a geographic area that is prone to flooding. During very rainy seasons, we will have some road closures. In these scenarios, students, parents and teachers become very anxious about bus cancellations or alternate routes to school. Our administration team communicates via phone messenger alerts, Remind alerts, email alerts, and social media posts so everyone is receiving immediate, specific feedback. No matter what the situation, put yourself in the place of others and use a tone that conveys honor and respect for the audiences receiving messages about changes.

For example, during one of our rainy seasons, we shared the message in figure 6.1 with parents via email.

Skiatook Schools Road Closures and Bus Routes

Parents and Guardians,

You should have received a district message by automated phone delivery that says:

> "Skiatook Schools will be open today. All bus routes will run with the exception of routes three and four. Route two will not pick up students east of Highway 11. We are sorry for the late notice but the safety of our students is our first concern."

Also, please note Highway 20 westbound is closed at present.

We will be patient with late arrivals as students find safe, alternate routes to school. Most important, please encourage student drivers to use only open routes. If a safe passage is not possible, students should stay at home until roads clear.

Respectfully,

Will Parker, Principal

Figure 6.1: Sample email to parents.

Also when you share statements with the press, convey a common message of honor to those watching outside of the school community. For example, our partnering career technology center offered to renovate classrooms at our high school and a neighboring high school for a new program offering. This investment to our schools will be significant. We collaborated with one of its directors on the press release in figure 6.2.

TULSA TECH OFFERS NEW CLASSES AT COLLINSVILLE & SKIATOOK HIGH SCHOOLS BEGINNING 2017–2018

TULSA, OK–February 1, 2017–Tulsa Tech will be offering two new classes on the campuses of Collinsville High School and Skiatook High School beginning school year 2017–2018. Introduction to Engineering and Principles of Engineering are courses that will help students explore lessons in S.T.E.M. (science, technology, engineering, and math).

Ninth-grade students enrolled in Introduction to Engineering will dig deep into the engineering design process, applying math, science, and engineering standards to hands-on projects. They work both individually and in teams to design solutions to a variety of problems using 3-D modeling software, and use an engineering notebook to document their work.

Tenth-grade students enrolled in Principles of Engineering will explore a broad range of engineering topics, including mechanisms, the strength of structures and materials, and automation. Students develop skills in problem solving, research, and design while learning strategies for design process documentation, collaboration, and presentation.

In partnership with both districts, Tulsa Tech has committed to providing a full-time instructor, who will teach mornings on one campus and afternoons on the other. In addition, Tulsa Tech is also renovating classroom spaces at both schools, as well as dedicating support for materials, technology, supplies, and curriculum.

For more information, students can talk to a high school counselor or Tulsa Tech advisor. For applications, visit tulsatech .edu or call 918-828-5000.

ABOUT TULSA TECH
Tulsa Tech, the oldest and largest in Oklahoma's CareerTech System, is a career and technology center school district dedicated to educating people for success in the workplace. Tulsa Tech helps high school and adult students from across the Tulsa region explore new careers, upgrade their training and skills, and pursue their dreams. More information can be found at tulsatech.edu.

Source: © 2017 Skiatook High School. Reprinted with permission.

Figure 6.2: Sample press release.

Embrace Social Media

Everyone wants to be the first to know important news, so learn how to use messaging tools effectively. Although you wouldn't want to share sensitive information using social media, you can use it for announcements, celebrations, and reminders. Some popular social media channels include Facebook, Twitter, LinkedIn, and Google+. Consider using students' social media tools as well. If they are using Instagram, then consider it a go-to tool at school as well. Social media outlets shouldn't replace traditional forms of public relations, such as press releases and newsletters, but it is hard to ignore their effectiveness given their ubiquitous nature in our culture. See chapter 7 (page 107) for specific ideas to use social media and other technology tools with parents' and community messaging.

Schools are complicated organizations with lots of moving parts. Although they don't usually market themselves like companies that provide merchandise or a service, schools do serve up something of value every day: education and care for the community's young people. Therefore, schools should be in the business of promoting positive messages by making good decisions, contextualizing, communicating with honor, and embracing social media as well as traditional outlets.

Now It's Your Turn

- If you had to give yourself and your teachers a grade for your public relations strengths and weaknesses, what would it be?

- In what areas can you improve? In what areas are you already successful?

Build a Platform for Communicating

The summer of my first year as high school principal, I was listening to a podcast on leadership when I heard a presentation by Michael Hyatt, a blogger, speaker, and author. Hyatt was once the chief executive officer of the publishing firm Thomas Nelson (LoCurto, 2012). During his last years with the publisher, he began blogging using a self-hosted WordPress site. As his readership grew, so did his influence. Eventually, he was attracting millions of readers to his website. In 2012, he published his book, *Platform: Get Noticed in a Noisy World*. After hearing his presentation, I bought his book. As I read it, I found myself stopping to add notes on the many ideas he had for sharing content, building an audience, and communicating consistently. Specifically, he described the ways leaders could leverage their messages through social media, using Twitter, Facebook, or blogs as platforms for sharing (Hyatt, 2012).

We live a world with lots of noise: technology, social media, advertising, and visual and sound media all compete for our attention. How are we to make sure our own messages are being heard in a world where so many are competing for attention? One point he made really stood out to me: Hyatt (2012) explained that he had been blogging for years without much readership. When he entered his fifth year of blogging, however, he saw an enormous surge in engagement. His lesson was that endurance, perseverance, and commitment to communication are just as important as the message you're delivering. In other words, as you commit to consistent, timely messaging, you build momentum over time. And others trust you as a reliable source of information (Hyatt, 2012).

If you want to make a difference in your school, your life, or the world, you must position yourself so that others can hear you. If you share your thoughts and ideas in a variety of ways, you increase your opportunity to influence others. After reading Hyatt's book, I decided to focus not only on messaging to my school but also platform building as a way to design and promote my messages inside and outside of my school.

Over the years, the tools I have used for this purpose have grown to include blogs, subscription-based emails, podcasts, website promotion, video, and webcasts. I started small, but the momentum has grown. Not only have I been able to increase my communication to my school community but I have also increased my communication with educators, specifically those in school leadership outside of my community. One example of a message that has resonated with my own school community as well as other school communities was a post I shared on my podcast and blog, "PMP: 052 Starting a Movement of Kindness" (Parker, 2017). In this post, I told the story I related in an earlier chapter about how girls were leaving positive notes on the mirror of a girls restroom until entire walls were covered with encouraging comments. After my post, I was contacted by Vicki Davis, a teacher who is also a blogger and podcaster, and was invited as a guest on her podcast, *10-Minute Teacher* (www.coolcatteacher.com/podcast), to share the story. When my interview went live, we shared the story with our teachers, students, and community as another reminder of the awesome ways our students are growing in character. (Visit www .coolcatteacher.com/kindness-goes-viral-mondaymotivation to listen to the conversation [Davis, 2017]).

These same digital tools work for communicating beyond your own community. For example, I was speaking to a group of teachers who were training to become principals. One of them asked me if I could share typical questions a candidate might encounter during an interview for a principal position. I decided to write a blog post, "30 Questions From Principal Interviews (Plus More)," to share with aspiring principals and post on my website (Parker, 2015b). I shared it as well on *Connected Principals* (http://connectedprincipals.com), a shared blog that education consultant and author George Couros hosts (Parker, 2015b). When I checked the blog statistics, that post had been downloaded 164,942 times (Parker, 2015b).

Not all principals enjoy writing, speaking, or content building. So as I share ideas on how to promote your message to the world, keep your own preferences in perspective. If you are not someone who enjoys the process of platform building, seek others in your building who have these gifts and talents that can help or support the ideas you want to communicate. As I added ways of platform building to my school routines, I found others who I could train to support the process. For instance, one member of our school staff takes all daily announcements and builds them into slides that we display throughout our school on big screens in common areas. I may help in shaping what messages we share, but she is responsible for the actual sharing on the big screens, as well as on social media and through text-message updates to parents.

Why is platform building so important? Here are some questions I want you to consider about building a platform beyond your school.

- Do you have ideas or beliefs about education that others can learn from and embrace to better serve students?

- Do you have lessons you can share to help other school leaders grow in their effectiveness?

- Do you wish to spread your school's message to others outside of your community?

If you answered yes to any of these questions, consider platform building to promote your core beliefs and values to others. In fact, I also believe that if school leaders do not build a platform of communication, others will fill the gap, and their message may not be the positive one you want to promote to others. Chapter 7 (page 107) provides specific technology tools to build a platform and to reach beyond your school to other learning communities and the world. Start by focusing on just one new tool or idea you could embrace to increase your own influence.

Partner With Parents

The medium you choose to use to communicate with parents is still not as important as the culture you create with consistent actions. As much as you might enjoy blogging or podcasting, the focus of messaging still comes back to the environment and expectations you set for your school.

With that in mind, ask yourself how you can design your communication so that you partner with parents to set positive expectations for student behavior. Messaging with parents while managing student behavior is just as important and powerful as providing information, celebrating, and platform building. Following are five suggestions for establishing strong messaging with parents about student behavior.

1. Be welcoming.

2. Communicate rewards and consequences.

3. Be firm, fair, and consistent.

4. Be polite, even when delivering bad news.

5. Be specific and document everything.

I discuss each of these suggestions in the following sections.

Be Welcoming

Before school begins each year, we hold a freshman orientation meeting for students and parents. We advertise this event in the local newspaper, on our website, through a principal newsletter, and via social media. As people arrive, we welcome them with music and colorful slides and images playing on a big screen. We introduce them to our administrative team, counselors, school sponsors, and representatives. Most important, they hear from older student leaders about what high school is all about. These orientation meetings are as important for the parents as they are for the students. Parents get an opportunity to hear from key adults in their children's lives, receive schedules and maps, tour the building, and ask questions. Inviting parents to the building allows face-to-face interaction as their first experience of our school. Starting off with a welcoming, informative, and productive time together communicates the kind of experience we want them to have all year long.

Communicate Rewards and Consequences

One of the reasons I like face-to-face interactions with parents and students is the opportunity to emphasize important conversations. As educators, we want every student to succeed, and we are here to partner with parents to do that. In addition to explaining expected behaviors, we put them in writing via our student handbook. We publish ahead of time the common responses to expected misbehaviors, and we predetermine consequences for infractions like unexcused absences, tardies, disruptive behavior, and so on. We share an abbreviated version of our conduct code with parents and post the entire handbook on our website. When explaining expected behaviors, here's a common rule of thumb: students' rewards for their good behavior are opportunities to learn and grow. Consequences for poor behavior will match the infraction. Parents and students deserve to know school is a safe place in which to learn, and you will partner together to keep school a productive place.

Be Firm, Fair, and Consistent

One of the worst lessons you can communicate is that there are no consequences for wrong choices. When you decide ahead of time the common expectations and consequences for an offense, it's easier to implement them consistently from student to student. Discipline must be firm, fair, and consistent if you are going to create an atmosphere of safe learning. Partnering with parents means keeping them informed. Also, celebrating the successes is important. For example, I was in class for a teacher observation. About halfway through the class, a student was answering questions when the teacher stopped and said, "Thank you for answering that question. I hope you know how much I appreciate how helpful you have been in class this school year." Later she told me that this student had been one of the most challenging students she had the year before. She noticed at the start of this school year that the student was trying harder to participate and be respectful, so the teacher decided to call the student's mother. When the mother answered, she expected bad news. Instead, the teacher shared a positive message. The parent was stunned, surprised, relieved, and encouraged. The teacher's expectations and consequences never changed, but her messaging in the process helped turn a challenging student situation into a successful one. The teacher's messaging, however, had begun a year earlier when she set expectations, enforced them consistently, and guided the student toward better choices. The fruit of her labors came with the new school year. Because this teacher was committed to clear, direct, but friendly interactions with this parent before and after the student transformation, the teacher became an ally to the parent in helping this student grow and mature. By communicating rewards and consequences, you set the tone for positive outcomes.

Be Polite, Even When Delivering Bad News

How do you greet students called into your office—especially when the reason is not a positive one? Make it a habit to welcome them. Greet them with a handshake or ask how they are doing. The same courtesy applies to parents. If educators and parents are to be partners, then leaders must treat them as equals—especially in situations that involve discipline issues and other bad news. Make a special effort to deliver the news in calm, polite terms. Ask yourself, "How would I want to receive this kind of information if I were in this parent's shoes?" Cultivate a reputation for staying calm and polite even in challenging moments.

Be Specific and Document Everything

In a world of litigation and policies, messaging and communication must include follow-through with good documentation. Documentation shows parents that you are consistent, thoughtful, and professional in how you deal with their children. When you administer discipline to a student and contact a parent, for example, make sure there is a record of the incident. Documentation serves three purposes: (1) it provides evidence of everything that you discuss or decide about a student, (2) it provides legal evidence that you have not violated anyone's right to due process, and (3) it makes clear to all parties involved exactly what the student must do to succeed. This documentation will become very helpful later for future situations in which it is critical to know important details of previous interactions. Although all this information remains confidential, these steps help maintain the positive message you want to communicate about expectations in your school.

Messaging with parents involves a mindset of treating students like you would want your own child to be treated. When parents and guardians feel like you still support students, even when correcting them, they are much more likely to want to be partners in improving student behavior. Of course, there will always be parents or guardians who disagree with you. It is especially important to err on the side of treating others with dignity in these situations. Messaging with parents is more than just what you share in a meeting, post on a website, or broadcast in media outlets; it also includes the small actions, conversations, and practices you implement with students every day. When you choose to focus on dignity and respect, you model what you want to see in others.

Finally, involve parents in the messaging of your school. Most parents and community members want to see their child's school promoted, so partner together. At the high school level, we use parent booster clubs to help support and promote activities. Our parent booster clubs include organizations such as Future Farmers of America, band, choir, baseball, basketball, football, volleyball, track and cross country, and wrestling, to name a few. When these organizations are holding fund-raisers or events, we publish their announcements in the school newsletter and attend their events. Likewise, parents will email or call me with updates, photos, or information that we can add to the positive messages we are sharing with the community. The cycle of messaging should involve all stakeholders: parents, teachers, students, administrators, and other community members. School leaders often see those outside the school building as critics of the school. You will never satisfy all your critics. But when you focus instead on the parents and community members who want what is best for students, and then you embrace all of these relationships as partnerships, not competitors, you will see your messaging consistently building in positive directions.

Now It's Your Turn

- In what ways have you learned to communicate with dignity even in difficult situations?

- What are some new steps you can take to positively partner with parents?

- When is your next event for parents? How can you organize that event with the perspective of someone coming to your building for the first time? What is one step you can take so that your messaging is positive, engaging, and encouraging for this event?

- What organizations or clubs can you encourage through your messaging so that students have more support and resources from their efforts?

Wrap Up

In May 2017, I attended the high school graduation commencement of my oldest daughter. The event began at 7 p.m. When the doors opened at 6 p.m., parents (mostly mothers) ran for open seats to hold for themselves and other friends or relatives they wanted sitting close to them. I was not only attending the graduation ceremony as a parent; I am my daughter's high school principal, so I would be on stage for the entire ceremony, but I wanted to say hello to my wife and other children before the ceremony began.

When I found the seats my wife was holding, I noticed that one parent had taped off a section of fifty seats. We do not allow people to tape off large sections of seating at our graduation ceremonies. I began removing tape, which was met by complaints from some parents and thanks from others. I then made my way backstage.

Later, my wife was talking to other parents as they waited for the start of the ceremony. She told me that one mom was upset that she couldn't tape off more seats. My wife said, "Yes, one of the challenges Will has in being a principal is that sometimes no matter what decision he makes, he often makes some people happy and other people upset." The mom quickly replied, "Yes, but he does such a good job otherwise so there are no hard feelings."

When you take time for messaging with your parents and community on a regular basis, the hard decisions you make are often judged in a more favorable light. This does not mean you will not face hard or challenging comments or feedback from community members. I still do. But it does mean that you are committed to being offensive, not defensive, when it comes to the messages from your school.

For example, prior to graduation ceremonies, I had been sending emails to parents in my weekly communications. I told parents about senior schedules, graduation practices, and reminders on our commencement ceremony. My team posted photos on social media of senior assemblies, spring concerts, and of seniors as they donned their caps and gowns and walked through elementary schools to the applause of younger children and former teachers. Our teachers and administrative team members attended their final events, and we practiced for two days with seniors on graduation commencement procedures. We had catered lunches for seniors and took a group photo of seniors in caps and gowns that we posted and shared. By the time we came to the big event, parents had already received lots of positive feedback from the school.

Parents have a vested interest in the value schools provide their children. I value the teachers and staff who have influenced my own daughter; however, if you are going to play a part in controlling the narratives others are hearing about your school, you must be committed to a consistent, relentless, positive, and strategic mindset of messaging. Just like students and teachers are influenced by your communication, the messaging your school shares also influences parents and community members. You are the chief communicator of the great opportunities and moments happening in your building. And the leadership you provide, decisions you make, and strategies you use in communicating go a long way in the opinions others hold of you and your school.

Using Technology to Message With Parents, the Community, and Beyond

Social media is not about the exploitation of technology but service to community.

—Simon Mainwaring

One of the most powerful communication tools is consistent, predictable outreach to parents, the community, and beyond. So what is a simple way to start? Before we begin looking at different tools for strategizing your messaging, take a look at what research says about technology use among most people in the United States. A 2016 report from Pew Research Center shows that 62 percent of U.S. adults get their news from social media sources. This number is up from 49 percent reported in 2012 (Gottfried & Shearer, 2016). Another Pew Research Report shows that 70 percent of people in the United States, Sweden, and Australia are consistently using social networking sites like Facebook and Twitter. People in countries with easy access to the Internet have higher usage of social media networks than people in less developed countries. These numbers also reveal that at least 30 percent of people in the United States do not rely on social media, but the trends show that number is decreasing with time (Poushter, 2017). With these numbers in mind, leaders cannot ignore that more and more of our parents and community members will rely on technology and devices for receiving your communication.

This chapter explores how to build a platform with technology and launch a school email campaign to make messaging with parents, the community, and beyond as far-reaching and successful as possible.

Build a Platform With Technology

As I discussed in chapter 6 (page 93), building a public relations platform is an important element of getting your message out to parents, the community, and beyond. Building a platform gives you the potential to reach as wide an audience as you choose. There are many technology tools available to help with this endeavor. In the following sections, I share those that I have used with great success as part of Skiatook's platform: blogs, podcasts, webinars, LinkedIn, Facebook, and Twitter.

Write Blog Posts

A blog is a webpage or website that an individual or organization regularly updates. They are usually conversational, often sharing personal information or opinions. According to Michael Hyatt (2012), most bloggers stop posting after their first or second year of blogging. He notes that it takes at least five years to build enough momentum and content to really establish an influential platform. When I began blogging, I committed to sharing at least one blog post a week for five years. As of writing this book, I am in year four of my blogging journey. I have a weekly schedule where I first upload my post and edit it as a draft. When it is ready to publish, I schedule the post to go out each week on Wednesday morning. Scheduling my posts for the same time each week allows others to anticipate my reliable, consistent source of information. Every week I write and publish five hundred to one thousand words, sharing ideas on learning and growing as a school leader, which has led to speaking engagements and the writing of this book. Of course, not everyone who blogs intends to share on a national or global scale. Many principals and school leaders successfully use blogging to update their audience on daily happenings in their schools, keep parents informed, or combine information with continuing education.

Blog entries for school leaders can be on a variety of topics. Here are some examples.

- How to prepare for the first days of school
- Books or articles on best practices in classrooms
- How new legislation may affect school services

- What new school programs or projects are upcoming
- Ways to stay inspired based on certain times of the year

Often I will write a blog post after being asked a specific question that requires thought and reflection before responding. Once a friend outside of my school asked me the most difficult question I had ever received as a principal: "In a meta-analysis of student data," he asked, "what would you say are the most significant factors in predicting student success?" He was an engineer, and he wanted to understand what processes educators used to predict student success. After fumbling for an answer, I rambled on about socioeconomic conditions of students and home environments as playing large roles. Later I decided it was time to do some research. What I discovered led me to a blog post by Grant Wiggins (2005) on John Hattie's (2009) book *Visible Learning: A Synthesis of Over 800 Meta-Analyses Relating to Achievement*. In a list of thirty-nine factors that significantly affect student progress, guess what factors ranked thirty-eight and thirty-nine? That's right, socioeconomic status and family background were at the bottom of the list (Wiggins, 2015). As a result, I decided it was time to write a blog post about the lessons I was still learning in my work as a career educator (Parker, 2015c). Blog posts do not have to be about research as some readers have other interests. The point is to think about posts that relate to work you are already doing in school that may benefit others if they knew more about it.

I do allow comments on my blog posts, and I have not had problems with inappropriate comments. For some reason, most people still like to email me questions or feedback instead of leaving comments. If you are interested in how to create a blog, Hyatt's (n.d.) *How to Launch a Self-Hosted WordPress Blog in 20 Minutes or Less* is very helpful. WordPress (https://wordpress.com) is only one site you can use to create a website or blog, but many school districts use WordPress to build their websites, so the format is familiar to many school leaders.

Create a Podcast

A podcast is an electronic audio file made available on the Internet that listeners can stream or download. Listeners can subscribe to a podcast to receive alerts when a new file is available.

Some popular education podcasts include:

- *The 10-Minute Teacher Podcast* by Vicki Davis
  (www.coolcatteacher.com/podcast)
- *EdChat Radio* with Tom Whitby and Nancy Blair
  (www.bamradionetwork.com/edchat-radio)
- *EduTalk* with David Noble and John Johnson
  (www.edutalk.info/category/radio-edutalk)
- *Every Classroom Matters*, Vicki Davis's longer podcast interviews
  (www.bamradionetwork.com/every-classroom-matters).

Jenn David-Lang, the founder of *The Main Idea* (www.themainidea
.net), sent me a list of her top-ten school leadership podcasts. I invited
her to post her thoughts on my blog in May 2016. Here is her list of
top school leadership podcasts (David-Lang, 2016).

- *Transformative Principal* with Jethro Jones
  (www.transformativeprincipal.org)
- *The School Leadership Show* with Mike Doughty
  (http://schoolleadershipshow.com)
- *School Principals Radio–NAESP Radio* with Gail Connelly
  (www.bamradionetwork.com/school-principals-radio)
- *School Administrators Radio–AASA Radio* with Dan Domenech
  (www.bamradionetwork.com/school-administrrors-radio)
- *Principally Speaking* with Jason Bodnar (https://itunes.apple
  .com/us/podcast/principally-speaking/id863595975?mt=2)
- *PrincipalPLN Podcast* with Spike Cook, Jessica Johnson, and
  Theresa Stager (http://principalpln.blogspot.com)
- *Principal Matters Podcast* with William D. Parker
  (www.williamdparker.com)
- *Principal Center Radio* with Justin Baeder
  (www.principalcenter.com/radio)
- *Educators Lead* with Jay Willis (www.educatorslead.com)
- *Better Leaders Better Schools* with Daniel Bauer
  (http://betterleadersbetterschools.com)

Many Friday mornings at Skiatook, senior student leaders gather in my office to record a podcast using GarageBand and my MacBook Pro. I convert the recording to an MP3 file, which I post on our school website or email to our superintendent of schools, teachers, or parents. I use a similar process to create a weekly podcast for school leaders— the *Principal Matters* podcast (www.williamdparker.com/?s=podcast). Podcasting is a little more complicated than just recording and sharing an MP3, however. If you want others to hear your podcast via iTunes, for instance, you must create a podcasting platform. For more information on learning to podcast, I recommend Pat Flynn's (2012) free tutorial *How to Start a Podcast: Pat's Complete Step-by-Step Podcasting Tutorial*. Flynn breaks down the process into six short videos.

If you decide to try podcasting, decide how often you want to share content, commit to that goal, and be consistent. I have created a weekly cycle for both my blogging and podcasting. Normally, I create content on Saturdays, and I have begun combining my blog posts and podcast. In this way, I can share written words as well as audio with people who like to listen to podcasts when commuting. Podcasting is a bit more complicated to set up than blogging, but the outcomes have been so encouraging in terms of listener downloads and feedback that it is well worth the effort.

Just like with blogging, podcast topics that may interest parents, teachers, or the community may include the following.

- Ways to answer questions all students have on the first days of school

- Strategies teachers are using to reach the hearts and smarts of students

- Steps the school is taking to implement a new program

- Interviews with teachers or students

- Special updates on successes of programs or initiatives

Host Webinars

Webinars allow people to come together online to share, collaborate, and learn. For example, I partnered with my state principals' association to launch a monthly *Brunch and Learn* webinar (www.ccosa.org/index .php?brunch-learn-leadership-webinars). We use a web-based video platform called Zoom (www.zoom.us). Zoom allows participants to join a conversation that I host from the office in my school. Participants can see my screen, and I can share elements of my screen with them. Plus, a video with audio appears in the corner of the screen so that viewers can see and hear the host, and the host can see and hear them if he or she chooses. Most times, participant microphones are automatically muted, but if someone has a question, the host can allow participants to unmute and talk. A scroll of monitors shows on the bottom of your screen with alternating faces of participants who have opted to video feed themselves into the chat. For example, in September 2016, fifty-four principals around the state of Oklahoma logged in for our first webinar conversation. When the webinar is over, Zoom automatically archives an MP4 recording (a compressed file) of the entire presentation so that those who missed it can log in later and view it. My state association office has a dedicated technology person who sets up a registration page for principals who want to participate. You can teach yourself to manage these platforms without assistance, but it is important to set up preferences ahead of time to mute participant microphones as well as record the session. The best part of this kind of platform is that it is free professional development, and no one has to leave his or her school to participate. Although lots of principals connect via video or phone, the webinar is still more of a straight presentation with time at the end for questions or comments. We had one hundred principals participate in the webcasts throughout one school year.

Following is a list of some topics from the *Brunch and Lunch* webinar series.

- **Organizational management:** How do you structure and assign key responsibility areas for your team to streamline the back end of learning? Are you ready for your accreditation report? Learn strategies on developing key responsibility areas and specific steps on how to plan for this year's accreditation report.

- **Purpose-driven leadership and goal setting:** What performance goals are you setting for your leadership team and yourself this year? What areas are you marking for your own evaluations? Revisit ideas on the importance of service-oriented motivation, discuss ways to stay focused without burnout, and learn ways to set BHAGs (big hairy audacious goals; Collins & Porras, 2004).

- **How to deal with difficult people:** What skills can you practice to manage difficult conversations with students, parents, or peers? Learn steps to follow when encountering stressful moments with others, and discover conflict-resolution strategies that de-escalate fired-up people. Discover how these same strategies work with your peers or coworkers.

Like webinars, you can also use other video-chatting formats other than Zoom. Try Google Hangouts, FaceTime, Facebook Live, or Skype to connect with other educators for live conversations. I have not used webinars to connect with parents or community members who are local, but I have talked to educators across the United States with these formats and have conducted a teacher interview through use of FaceTime.

Use LinkedIn

LinkedIn (www.linkedin.com) is a networking tool that allows users to build a network of professional contacts from across the United States and even the world. Once you build a profile page on LinkedIn, the website identifies professionals who have similar interests with whom you may want to connect. It is not as social or casual as Facebook, but it has two options that could help you promote strong messaging: (1) updates and (2) articles. If you find an interesting piece of writing, video, or resource, it is easy to copy the link and share it as an update on LinkedIn for your contacts to see. LinkedIn also allows you to write posts or articles similar to blog posts. The site catalogues these posts under your profile so that others who visit your page can see what information or ideas you value. When I find an interesting article or story, I may share it via LinkedIn, Twitter, Facebook, or my blog. Because each tool reaches a slightly different set of individuals, the ability to share information and find valuable resources increases. I can also connect with other education professionals, teachers, or parents who have LinkedIn profiles. One tip I have for users of multiple social media platforms is this: repurpose your content. For example, if you have an interesting blog post you have written about best practices happening in your school, repost the same article via your school's Facebook page, Twitter feed, and your LinkedIn account. The more exposure your school receives from multiple platforms, the better.

Use Facebook

Having a school Facebook public site is a great way for parents to check on what is happening in schools. Facebook has many advantages for social media sharing. You can upload multiple photos or videos. You can tag photos by connecting the faces of teachers or students back to a family member's Facebook account. You can post invitations to events. And you can boost posts if you want to increase exposure of a story or announcement. For just a few dollars, you can set up preferences in Facebook to publish a story to thousands or millions of other users. I mentioned in chapter 4 (page 61) that we boosted a Facebook post about our wall of kindness in the girls bathroom, and that post had over sixty-five thousand impressions. Know your school's procedures on student privacy and make sure your parents agree to student information or photo sharing before publicizing individual student photos.

Use Twitter

By far one of my favorite tools for quick sharing of information is Twitter. It is a popular tool—many school leaders, parents, and community members use it, and you can message individual users directly; a phone number or email address isn't necessary in order to connect. Twitter users can tweet (send out) messages up to 140 characters from a registered account. Hashtags (abbreviations that begin with the # sign) organize tweets by topic. When you type a hashtag into the search bar on Twitter, you find conversations within the hashtag category.

Twitter has also become one of the best platforms for instant sharing of student learning or success. By including a direct link @SkiatookSchools, my tweets are automatically shown on our school's Twitter page and show as a feed on the district website. For example, one night I was watching a high school varsity girls' basketball game that was tied going into the last seconds of the game. I decided to use Twitter's live feed app called Periscope. As soon as I began broadcasting through this app on my iPhone, I could see icons of parents and students liking the feed and watching the live feed of the game as it ended. Twitter is also a great way to rally around an event by sharing a common hashtag. Another example is when our school student leaders organized a weeklong fund-raising campaign. Our school mascot is the bulldog, so they used the hashtag #Barkweek2K17 to promote the events. Two hundred and seven parents, teachers, and friends followed the week's events online (https://twitter.com/Barkweek2K17). Figure 7.1 is a screenshot of the Twitter page our student council sponsor and students created for the event.

Source: © 2017 Skiatook High School. Reprinted with permission.

Figure 7.1: Twitter page for Bark Week.

One of Twitter's most valuable features for educators is the opportunity to participate in chats. For instance, committed groups of educators across the United States gather on specific days of the week to talk about issues in education. Some of my favorite hashtags include #edchat, #satchat, #leadupchat, #atplc, and #leadered. Even though Twitter limits messages to 140 characters or fewer, you can find all kinds of gems of information or links to great articles to encourage your growth as a school leader. Within my school community, we also use the hashtag #shsrednation so that anytime I make a post about my students or school events, I can inform others who look for that hashtag. Educator and author John Wink has promoted a Love My School Day on Twitter. Educators are encouraged to take photos, videos, and leave comments about their schools and use the hashtag #LoveMySchoolDay. This Twitter event has become so popular that the hashtag shows as trending on Twitter's list of top tweets throughout the day. I often spend time reading through posts by other principals, and it is so encouraging to see the amazing moments happening in schools across the United States.

Platform building is a powerful way to enhance messaging. Technology tools can help you consistently and effectively share messages that reach parents, your school community, and beyond. When I think back to the time I read Hyatt's (2012) book, *Platform*, little did I know that a few years later, platform building would allow me to share my own ideas with people from across the United States and around the world. Whether your messages are targeting your local community or broadcasting to the world, you have so many tools available for spreading the great news of what is happening in schools.

Now It's Your Turn

- What is one new way in which you can commit to sharing your own lessons in leadership?

- In what ways can you spread the news about practical examples of learning, leading, or instructing going on in your school?

- If you had to choose a tool for practicing platform building, which one would most interest you? Share those ideas with another school leader for feedback.

Launch a School Email Campaign

Email is a tool most, if not all, teachers and parents are adept with. Individuals and teams prefer it for communication within the school, but it can also help you easily reach a large number of parents and school community members with ease.

In 2013 a team member at our school suggested I start emailing parents regular updates. I started by using a list exported from our student information system. The effort soon turned into a habit, and I began receiving more positive feedback than I had seen with any other communication effort.

My weekly email campaign to parents was difficult at first because of the limitations of my school email account, which limits one-time sends to five hundred addresses. For a large email list, you may find a subscription email program like MailChimp (https://mailchimp.com) to be helpful. This free email service sends mass emails for up to two thousand users. There are other subscription-based email programs to choose from, but because I use MailChimp, I'll describe my email campaign process using this program for illustrative purposes.

To start, create an account for a subscription-based email service such as MailChimp. The site will ask for a website address to which it can direct users. I suggest using your school website address as your homepage. MailChimp's site tutorial helps you create a system that is easy to edit week to week. Plus, if you use the following tips, you can archive each week's updates on your school website.

Once you have an account, log in. The site will prompt you to follow instructions to upload your existing email list. You can either enter addresses by hand or upload them via an Excel document. To share additional content, there are several options. You can create a newsletter as a Word document, save it as a PDF, and upload it to your school website to create a URL. This is how I produce my newsletters. Or, you can manage your additional content directly through MailChimp using the free templates the site provides. Others have simply updated a blog page as a web-based newsletter.

Then you can get started building your first email campaign. Using MailChimp's Create-a-Campaign step-by-step menu, choose a template for the email, compose a message, and if you have other websites or student newsletters to share, insert the links in your email campaign.

Following MailChimp's tutorial, schedule a time to launch the email to everyone on your list. Figures 7.2 and 7.3 (page 118) show an email to parents and a sample template option. Figure 7.4 (page 119) shows a sample newsletter.

> ## Newsletter Updates
>
> Dear Parents and Guardians,
>
> You are receiving this email because you have subscribed to receive updates from _____. If you do not wish to receive these updates, use the link at the bottom of this page to unsubscribe.
>
> By clicking on the following link, you can access this week's newsletter. Feel free to share it with others!
>
> Click here for latest update:
>
> **LINK TO YOUR NEWSLETTER HERE**
>
> Thanks again for the opportunity to serve your students.
>
> Sincerely,
>
> _____

Figure 7.2: Email campaign template letter to parents.

*Visit **go.SolutionTree.com/leadership** to download a free reproducible version of this figure.*

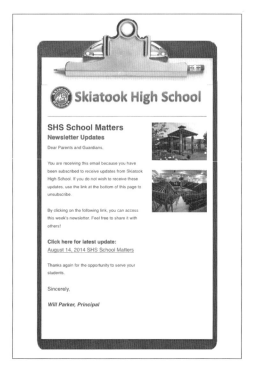

Source: © 2017 Skiatook High School. Reprinted with permission.

Figure 7.3: Sample template design for email campaign letter to parents.

Source: © 2017 Skiatook High School. Reprinted with permission.

Figure 7.4: Sample newsletter for parents.

Finally, create a subscription sign-up button to post on the school's website. Within MailChimp's tutorials, locate the hypertext markup language (HTML) code to paste onto your school website so visitors can subscribe to receive the email campaign.

The benefits of using a service like MailChimp for your email campaign include tracking the numbers of emails opened, deleting duplicates, and alerting you to new subscribers. The downsides include the possibility that users' email services will automatically quarantine the mass email or move it out of the recipient's in-box. To remedy this, I send out a heads-up email from my personal email account to alert recipients to expect messages from an alternate account and to check their spam folders for my letter.

I do not consider myself a natural with technology; it's actually hard work for me. But I like to learn systems that can optimize communication to my school community. If you want to increase your email reach and communicate regularly and effectively with parents, using a mass email system like MailChimp is a positive step in this direction.

- How can you tie a subscription-based email list into the networks or websites your school already has in place?

- Is there someone on your team who can handle the technical aspects of a campaign?

- How can you play an active role in deciding what positive news you should share that matches your school's mission, vision, and goals?

Publicize Celebration

Finding creative ways to celebrate and publicize the positive behaviors students show in school on a daily basis is an excellent way to share positive messages about your school with parents, and technology tools make this sharing easier than ever before. For example, our student council launched plans to award a Class Cup to the grade of students who showed the most participation in good deeds and school spirit throughout the school year. Similar to the fictional school Hogwarts from the *Harry Potter* book series, students earn points as a group (in our case, grades 9, 10, 11, and 12 rather than by Gryffindor, Ravenclaw, Hufflepuff, and Slytherin). The class that earns the most points receives a trophy and bragging rights at the end of the school year.

Throughout the campaign, teachers submit good deed notices through a shared Google Form. They report students for deeds like working hard on an assignment, helping classmates with lessons, opening the door for others, volunteering to pick up trash, or planting flowers in front of the school. Student council members deliver good deed awards to classes, and we share photos of students via our social media platforms for teachers and parents to see.

Student council members help plan the steps they follow to introduce the Class Cup idea, track points among students, and recognize merits as the momentum builds. As you're thinking about digital tools for messaging, consider these three simple strategies and tools from our Class Cup strategy.

Create a Promotional Video

At our first school pep assembly, the student council officers explained the Class Cup (n.d.) contest and showed a great promotional video to introduce the idea (http://bit.ly/2vwo6tR). They created the video with the help of a faculty advisor using Biteable (https://biteable.com), a free video creator. Because many students are such visual learners, a video promotional is a great way to introduce a new idea or initiative, and with easy-to-use online resources, it is fun to create. Afterward, you can share the video with parents via school newsletters, blog about it, or share with others via Twitter, LinkedIn, or Facebook.

Collect Data

Our student council faculty sponsor followed up the students' presentation with a presentation to faculty on how the Class Cup process would work. She created a process for tracking the large number of students who may be reported for good deeds. After identifying students who deserve recognition for a good deed, a teacher submits the student's name via a Google Form, which links to a Google spreadsheet, automatically updating it. You can design the Google Form to include whatever information you want to capture, such as student name, student's class, and a description of the student's good deed.

Google has some easy-to-use functions as part of Google Drive. You can share documents, spreadsheets, or forms on a Google Drive and allow others to have access to them and edit what you post there. Google Docs allow multiple people (like an entire faculty) to access and edit the same document. A Google Form is a shared document one person can create that other users can fill in anytime to update information. All the data is collected in one document where it is easy to review information or tabulate points. As the Google spreadsheet automatically captures information, it populates a class-points list. Figure 7.5 (page 122) shows an example.

Google Forms is a practical way to capture teacher-reported data. Whether you are in a school with one hundred students or twenty-five hundred students, these forms allow immediate tracking and tabulating of data. Best of all, they are free.

	A	B	C	D	E
1					
2	Point Producers	Freshmen	Sophomores	Juniors	Seniors
3	Good Deeds	210	240	200	185
4	Pep Assembly 9/9/16	—	—	—	10
5	Pep Assembly 9/16/16	5	—	5	5
6	Hallway Decorations	—	—	15	—
7	Spirit Day Dress Up	3	12	—	—
8	Scavenger Hunt	5	20	—	10
9	Tardies (First Nine Weeks)	20	10	30	40
10	Dress Code (First Nine Weeks)	20	10	40	30
11	Book Drive	—	—	—	25
12	Door Decorations	10	—	10	—
13	Pep Assembly 11/9/16	10	—	—	—
14	Turkey Challenge	50	—	—	—
15	Tardies (Second Nine Weeks)	40	30	20	10
16	Dress Code (Second Nine Weeks)	20	10	30	40
17	**Totals**	**393**	**332**	**350**	**355**

Source: © 2017 Skiatook High School. Reprinted with permission.

Figure 7.5: Sample of automatically tallied form.

Provide Consistent Recognition

As students demonstrate noteworthy behaviors throughout the school, use daily announcements to celebrate. Deliver good deed award certificates to students in front of peers each morning. See figure 7.6 for an example of an award. When students receive awards, a teacher or student council member takes a photo, and we include recognitions in weekly emails to parents and on our school Facebook site. Our local newspaper editor also subscribes to my parent email campaigns, and she will often republish photos and information both online and in print.

At the end of our first year of publishing good deeds and tabulating Class Cup points, the class officers of the grade with the most points received a large trophy and we shared photos and announcements via email and on our school's social media platforms too. Figure 7.7 (page 124) is a sample email that went out about the winners. When you have the mindset to look for positive deeds and students know it, you will see students act with kindness or generosity every day. Celebrating such deeds helps normalize these behaviors, and sharing recognition through technology makes it easy for school leaders to reach parents and the community. If we spend more time correcting poor behavior than recognizing good deeds, we run the risk of missing out on the kinds of behaviors we want to spotlight in our schools. In the end, positive behavior is contagious, and these are the kind of messages you want parents, community members, and the world to hear and see about your school.

GOOD DEED AWARD

Congratulations,

_____!

Your good deed has been reported and you have earned your class five points toward the Class Cup! Thank you for being a great example for the students at Skiatook High School!

Good deed: _____

Reported by: _____

Figure 7.6: Daily good deed award certificate.

Visit go.SolutionTree.com/leadership to download a free reproducible version of this figure.

Class Cup Winners 2016–2017

Skiatook High School has announced the freshman class as the SHS Class Cup winners for 2016–2017.

The Class Cup was a yearlong competition hosted by student council where students earned points for their classes by showing school spirit, participation in events, and good behavior. Also students earned points when reported by teachers for doing good deeds.

Throughout the school year, teachers submitted over one hundred seventy good deeds for students who were seen displaying good behavior in some way. Here are just ten of the comments from teachers who submitted nominations:

- "My sub on Friday pointed out that Hailey went out of her way to help a fellow student who became stressed out and walked out of class. She helped calm him down, brought him back, and helped him finish his quiz."
- "Since school has started, Dalton gets up every time papers are turned in and gathers them for me. I've never asked him, but he does this every day. It's respectful and helpful."
- "On several occasions I have found Carlos holding the door open for students during passing periods and at the end of the day."
- "Sarah voluntarily planted flowers in the garden area of the main building between the ninth-grade building."
- "Evan found a purse that a girl had left on a table at the end of lunch and handed it in so it could be returned."
- "Carey donated some pencils to help students that didn't have any."
- "After the PreACT was over, Darren asked me if there was anything he could do to help me. It was super appreciated!!!"
- "Xavier volunteered to do partner work with one of my more challenging students with a positive attitude and no complaints."
- "Laney solved a particularly difficult technological issue that was preventing me from making a presentation to the class by using her problem-solving skills."

Figure 7.7: Sample email for Class Cup winners.

So proud of all SHS students for making this a great year of positivity, school spirit, and excellence!

Attached is a photo of freshman class officers Braden Best and Jayden Garner (left to right) holding the coveted cup for their class!

Sincerely,

Will Parker, Principal

Host a Fund-Raiser to Finish Strong

As I mentioned in the section on Twitter, our student leadership class also launched a final campaign to end the school year with positivity. They created a campaign called BARK Week. The students came up with the name, an acronym for "Bulldogs Achieving Real Kindness." Through a series of events, they raised donations for Pearl's Hope in Tulsa, Oklahoma—a ten-month transition home for homeless women and their children, so they do not have to be separated. This was another great way to encourage celebration with an outward focus. In some ways, it was the culmination of an entire year of promoting good deeds as the students took their ideas for helping others into the community. In one week, they raised over $1,500 for the shelter.

Now It's Your Turn

- How could you use Biteable or Google Forms to enhance your messaging about student behavior with others?

- What are some ways you can promote the great deeds happening throughout your school?

Wrap Up

Have you ever had this conversation with a child?

"How was school today?"

"OK. I guess."

"Anything interesting happen?"

"No, not really."

"Anything I need to know about coming up at school."

"Not that I know of."

I am a father of four. My wife and I have three teenage daughters and a preteen son. As a career educator, I have spent a lot of time with teens. But as a father, I have discovered something about my own children that confirms what other parents have told me for years: our children don't always tell us what we need to know about what is happening at school. School leaders have a platform that others do not. So take advantage of the platform.

My school has a lot of students who play sports or compete in activities like art, drama, music, or speech. Whenever a coach or director is preparing his or her team for a big event, he or she will often think of what to say to convey the importance of every player's focus, commitment, courage, and actions. "This is your moment," he or she may say. "This is what you have been working so hard to achieve. Every practice, every grueling workout, every win and loss have prepared you for this."

You may be working hard to encourage a positive culture of learning within your school, but there is often a gap of communication that exits between schools and parents. Frankly, if this gap continues, you have missed an opportunity to bring learning full circle. If community members or others outside our schools fail to understand what is happening in our schools, then you have missed an opportunity to influence the conversation about your school. If the general public fails to know that your school is doing amazing work with students, then the general misperceptions of schools may continue.

As a school leader, you have the unique position of seeing the bigger picture. And you have a platform that no one else has. This is your moment. You have been pouring your heart and soul into providing great opportunities for student learning and achievement. You spend hours engaged in supporting, encouraging, counseling, and managing others. Don't let the amazing work happening among your teachers and students go unnoticed. With the right strategies, tools, and actions, you can use your platform to take back the conversation people are having about your school.

EPILOGUE
Messaging Tips

*In a world of constant change, the
fundamentals are more important than ever.*

—Jim Collins

I played basketball as a child. And over the years, as a teacher, parent, and principal, I have watched a lot of games. Sometimes I'll still shoot baskets with my children until my legs give out and they're asking me if they should call 911. One summer, my two older daughters were practicing for summer league basketball, and my parental duty was to taxi them to practices or games and watch a lot of messy basketball.

One afternoon, I observed my daughter repeating the same mistakes over and over again when playing offense. So I jotted down some pointers to share with her that evening over burritos. Later, I began to think through how these basketball tips also apply to our own performance as school leaders—especially as it relates to communication. How do your practices, mindsets, and commitments to messaging create the kind of positive entanglements you want to see happening in your school community? Maybe the following tips will help you as you think about how messaging can improve your service to your students, teachers, parents, and the world.

Get Open

To *get open* means to understand that everyone has an integral part to play. Strong teams do not work if team members are happy bystanders. As a school leader, have you decided where you want to move the ball in your area of responsibility? Have you chosen practical steps and tools for improving your messaging? Improvement starts with one good move, but you first have to be open minded so you're ready to take advantage of the best moments. Just like in basketball, if you do not stay committed to taking personal action in making something happen, you are simply wasting time.

Talk to Your Teammates

Communication is the key for any strong team. Pull together often as team members to compare notes. In schools, educators communicate both formally and informally. Throughout the chapters of this book, you have learned that no matter what tools you choose for communication, you cannot survive on your own island of work. You need your team, and each team member needs you. So talk regularly about what each of you needs to accomplish. And then work together toward that end.

Offer Assistance

Even the most talented basketball player can get trapped if her defenders double-team her. In schools, none of us are superheroes. Each of us faces tasks or situations that may be bigger than we are. During those times, we need one another's support. Seasoned teachers must support new ones. School leaders must provide resources and support for all their team members. Communication is no different. How can you build a culture in which everyone steps in to help one another with messaging? This doesn't mean doing each other's jobs. It means providing the needed assistance, resources, or moral support during tough times.

Anticipate

If you are familiar with the game of basketball, you know a good pass doesn't just happen. Rarely do players have much time to launch clean, unobstructed passes to one another. In schools, you will rarely get the luxury of providing instruction or communication without conflict, challenges, distractions, or frustrations. If you are committed to schoolwide success, then you anticipate these challenges and plan ahead. For example, when a team member is working on a task that you know requires assistance, run to help. Don't wait for your colleague to ask. When you want to frequently communicate with parents or team members, plan for it. For instance, I have a running commitment to send out a parent newsletter every Thursday. I have built all my goals for that deadline with Thursday afternoon in mind. The same goes for times I schedule leadership meetings, faculty meetings, or classroom visits. Working with other team members will help accomplish your goals. One summer before school began, an assistant principal and I sat down and listed over twenty important tasks that we still needed to complete for a successful start of school. Good teamwork is more than just a simple equation; good teams provide exponential results.

Identify Strengths and Opportunities

I once attended a presentation by veteran educator and author Harry Wong, who said, "It is okay to admit you are the expert" (H. Wong, personal communication, November 1998). In basketball, you must lean into your strengths to position yourself to take advantage of opportunities. No matter what obstacles you face, your training, background, education, and experiences have made you capable of winning in the classroom or the schoolhouse. The same applies in communicating about schoolwide initiatives. Lean into your strengths so that you will stay effective during challenging times. You won't be able to implement every tip, tool, or idea in this book. But if you can master something new this week, this month, or this year, you are showing continual growth—which is really what can eventually make anyone an expert in education.

Stay in Control

In basketball, your strategy cannot be, "How can I get rid of this ball?" It should be, "What can I make happen with this ball?" Good execution requires taking responsibility for the outcome, and so does effective instruction and leadership. Strong educators teach with both sides of their brains at once. Or as I sometimes think of it, they teach with both hands at once. In other words, you instruct based on the content you know (on the one hand), and you manage behavior so that students can understand and learn (with the other hand). This two-sided approach to learning applies in all aspects of school life. You control the ball by creating the best environment possible for learning to take place. Then you execute with the best strategies. The same is true with messaging. You do not give up the best practices you have always implemented so that you can try new ways of messaging. Instead, you continue doing what works while attempting ways to enhance, increase, or improve on what works.

No matter how many times I have watched my own children play basketball, I find myself watching them more than anyone else's children. If you are a parent, it is no surprise that you have a difficult time separating your own sense of accomplishment from the successes or failures you observe in your children. Our entanglements are powerful and mysterious motivators. I believe that just as parents are mysteriously entangled with the ups and downs of their own children, school leaders are entangled with the successes and failures of their schools. Will you choose to be on the offensive when it comes to your school's messaging? There are no magic formulas for success in sports or in messaging. In both settings, success happens more often when you practice the basics. Playing offense means strategizing to win, not just surviving until the end of the game. As you look at the road ahead in your school leadership, remember to play smart, communicate often, provide support, stay proactive, position yourself wisely, and implement actions strategically. When you do, your messaging may become a game changer for inspiring teachers, motivating students, and reaching communities.

Now It's Your Turn

- What is one new action you can take today as the chief communicator for your school?

- What will be your first step toward turning your community members into raving fans of your school's successes?

REFERENCES AND RESOURCES

Andreatta, B. (2017). *Wired to resist: The brain science of why change fails and a new model for driving success.* Santa Barbara, CA: 7th Mind.

Baldoni, J. (2002, April 1). Effective leadership communications: It's more than talk. *Harvard Management Communication Letter, 5*(4), 3–5.

Bryant, J. (2015, April 24). *Tony Robbins quotes: His 75 most motivational lines* [Blog post]. Accessed at http://selfmadesuccess.com/tony-robbins -quotes-motivational on December 22, 2016.

Canfield, J., Hansen, M. V., & Kirberger, K. (1997). *Chicken soup for the teenage soul: 101 stories of life, love, and learning.* Deerfield Beach, FL: Health Communications.

Casas, J. (2016, July 30). *Wherever you are going, you are almost there* [Blog post]. Accessed at www.jimmycasas.com/wherever-you-are-going-you-are -almost-there on July 31, 2016.

Chapman, G. (1995). *The five love languages: How to express heartfelt commitment to your mate.* Chicago: Northfield.

Choi, C. Q. (2015, March 27). *Quantum record! 3,000 atoms entangled in bizarre state.* Accessed at www.livescience.com/50280-record -3000-atoms-entangled.html on April 1, 2015.

Class Cup. (n.d.). *Class Cup promotional video* [Video file]. Accessed at https://biteable.com/watch/class-cup-promotional-video-508274/5cd3881 6d94f189c25a18231d6bb5fafd6379bde on August 4, 2017.

Collins, J. (2001). *Good to great: Why some companies make the leap . . . and others don't.* New York: HarperBusiness.

Collins, J. C., & Porras, J. I. (2004). *Built to last: Successful habits of visionary companies.* New York: HarperBusiness.

Covey, S. R. (1989). *The seven habits of highly effective people: Restoring the character ethic.* New York: Simon & Schuster.

David-Lang, J. (2016, May 18). *Top 10 school leadershop podcasts* [Blog post]. Accessed at www.williamdparker.com/2016/05/18/top-10-school-leadership-podcasts on July 25, 2017.

Davis, V. (2017, April 10). *When kindness goes viral* [Audio podcast]. Accessed at www.coolcatteacher.com/kindness-goes-viral-mondaymotivation on May 21, 2017.

DuFour, R. (2015). *In praise of American educators: And how they can become even better.* Bloomington, IN: Solution Tree Press.

DuFour, R., DuFour, R., Eaker, R., Many, T. W., & Mattos, M. (2016). *Learning by doing: A handbook for Professional Learning Communities at Work* (3rd ed.). Bloomington, IN: Solution Tree Press.

Elmore, T. (2015). *Generation iY: Secrets to connecting with today's teens & young adults in the digital age.* Atlanta, GA: Poet Gardener.

Flynn, P. (2012, October 22). *How to start a podcast: Pat's complete step-by-step podcasting tutorial.* Accessed at www.smartpassiveincome.com/how-to-start-a-podcast-podcasting-tutorial on September 24, 2016.

Gallup. (2013). *State of the American workplace: Employee engagement insights for U.S. business leaders.* Washington, DC: Author.

Godin, S. (2009, August 15). *Willfully ignorant vs. aggressively skeptical* [Blog post]. Accessed at http://sethgodin.typepad.com/seths_blog/2009/08/willfully-ignorant-vs-aggressively-skeptical.html on December 22, 2016.

Gordon, J. (2013, December 30). *20 tips for a positive new year: Updated for 2014* [Blog post]. Accessed at www.jongordon.com/positive-tip-positive-new-year-2014.html on January 15, 2014.

Gottfried, J., & Shearer, E. (2016, May 26). *News use across social media platforms 2016.* Accessed at www.journalism.org/2016/05/26/news-use-across-social-media-platforms-2016 on May 20, 2017.

Hanson, E. (2015, June 10). *Communication skills for leaders* [Blog post]. Accessed at https://hunet.harding.edu/wordpress/magazine/2015/06/10/communication-skills-for-leaders on December 22, 2016.

Hattie, J. (2009). *Visible learning: A synthesis of over 800 meta-analyses relating to achievement.* London: Routledge.

Heffernan, M. (2015, May). *Margaret Heffernan: Forget the pecking order at work* [Video file]. Accessed at www.ted.com/talks/margaret_heffernan_why_it_s_time_to_forget_the_pecking_order_at_work on May 12, 2017.

Hull, J. (2012, April). *The principal perspective: Full report.* Alexandria, VA: Center for Public Education. Accessed at www.centerforpubliceducation.org/principal-perspective on March 16, 2016.

Hyatt, M. (n.d.). *How to launch a self-hosted WordPress blog in 20 minutes or less: A step-by-step guide.* Accessed at https://michaelhyatt.com/ez-wordpress-setup.html on September 24, 2016.

Hyatt, M. (2012). *Platform: Get noticed in a noisy world.* Nashville, TN: Nelson.

Juliani, A. J. (2016, May). *The beginner's guide to design thinking in the classroom.* Accessed at http://ajjuliani.com/the-beginners-guide-to-design-thinking-in-the-classroom on February 22, 2017.

LoCurto, C. (2012, May 22). *Personal selling with Michael Hyatt.* Dave Ramsey's Entre Leadership Podcast. Accessed at http://entreleadershippodcast.entreleadership.libsynpro.com/personal-selling-with-michael-hyatt on May 20, 2017.

MailChimp. (2017, May 1). *Getting started with Mailchimp.* Accessed at http://kb.mailchimp.com/accounts/account-setup/getting-started-with-mailchimp on May 20, 2017.

McNulty, R. J., & Quaglia, R. J. (2007). Rigor, relevance and relationships. *School Administrator, 64*(8), 18–23. Accessed at www.aasa.org/SchoolAdministratorArticle.aspx?id=6534 on May 18, 2017.

Miller, L., & Spiegel, A. (Hosts). (2015, January 30). *Entanglement* [Audio podcast]. Accessed at www.npr.org/programs/invisibilia/382451600/entanglement?showDate=2015–01–30 on April 1, 2015.

Nyad, D. (2013, December). *Diana Nyad: Never, ever give up* [Video file]. Accessed at www.ted.com/talks/diana_nyad_never_ever_give_up?language=en on January 15, 2014.

Parker, W. D. (2014). *Principal matters: The motivation, courage and action needed for school leadership.* Owasso, OK: Author.

Parker, W. D. (2015a, April 1). *The power of "entanglement": Implications for school leaders* [Blog post]. Accessed at www.williamdparker.com/2015/04/01/the-power-of-entanglement-implications-for-school-leaders on September 17, 2016.

Parker, W. D. (2015b, March 25). *30 questions from principal interviews (plus more)* [Blog post]. Accessed at www.williamdparker.com/2015/03/25/30-questions-from-principal-interviews-plus-more on May 20, 2017.

Parker, W. D. (2015c, November 11). *What factors predict student success?* [Blog post]. Accessed at www.williamdparker.com/2015/11/11/what-factors-predict-student-success on May 20. 2017.

Parker, W. D. (2017, February 1). *PMP 052: Starting a movement of kindness* [Blog post]. Accessed at www.williamdparker.com/2017/02/01/pmp-052-starting-a-movement-of-kindness on May 20, 2017.

Payne, R. K. (2005). *A framework for understanding poverty* (4th rev. ed.). Highlands, TX: aha! Process.

Poushter, J. (2017, April 20). *Not everyone in advanced economies is using social media.* Accessed at www.pewresearch.org/fact-tank/2017/04/20/not-everyone-in-advanced-economies-is-using-social-media on May 20, 2017.

Ramsey, D. (2011). *Entreleadership: 20 years of practical business wisdom from the trenches.* New York: Howard Books.

Risseghem, J. V. (2009, August 28). *Oral Roberts University sees increase in enrollment for fall 2009.* Accessed at www.oru.edu/news/oru_news/20090828_enrollment_increase_release.php on May 20, 2017.

Saenz, A. L. (2012). *The power of a teacher: Restoring hope and well-being to change lives.* Glebe, Australia: Intermedia.

Skiatook Public Schools. (n.d.a). *FridayAnnouncments090916* [Audio file]. Accessed www.skiatookschools.org/fridayannouncments090916 on August 4, 2017.

Skiatook Public Schools. (n.d.b). *Newsletter updates: SHS newsletter updates.* Accessed www.skiatookschools.org/schools/skiatook-high-school/principal-newsletter on August 4, 2017.

Tulsa Public Schools. (2015). *TLE observation and evaluation rubric: Teachers.* Accessed at www.tulsaschools.org/4_About_District/_documents/TLE/Observation_Evaluation_Rubric_Teachers.pdf on March 18, 2015.

Whitaker, T. (2012). *Shifting the monkey: The art of protecting good people from liars, criers, and other slackers.* Bloomington, IN: Solution Tree Press.

Wiggins, G. (2015, February). *What works in education—Hattie's list of the greatest effects and why it matters.* Accessed at https://grantwiggins.wordpress.com/2012/01/07/what-works-in-education-hatties-list-of-the-greatest-effects-and-why-it-matters on May 20, 2017.

Wong, H. K., & Wong, R. T. (1998). *The first days of school: How to be an effective teacher.* Mountain View, CA: Wong.

Wong, H. K., & Wong, R. T. (2000). There is only one first day of school. *Teacher.net Gazette.* Accessed at http://www.teachers.net/wong/AUG00/wongprint.html on May 18, 2017.

INDEX

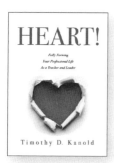

HEART!
Timothy D. Kanold
Use this resource to reflect on your professional journey and discover how to foster productive, heart-centered classrooms and schools.
BKF749

From Leading to Succeeding
Douglas Reeves
Utilizing the elements of effective leadership—purpose, trust, focus, leverage, feedback, change, and sustainability—education leaders can overcome any challenge.
BKF649

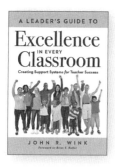

A Leader's Guide to Excellence in Every Classroom
John R. Wink
Explore the Hierarchy of Instructional Excellence and schoolwide support systems to help education leaders guarantee ultimate teacher success.
BKF719

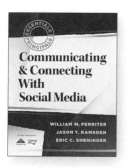

Communicating & Connecting With Social Media
William M. Ferriter, Jason T. Ramsden, and Eric C. Sheninger
Transform your communication practice. Learn how administrators can use social media to communicate with staff, students, parents, and other stakeholders.
BKF474

GL⦿BAL PD

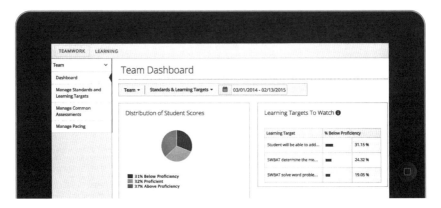

The **Power to Improve** Is in Your Hands

Global PD gives educators focused and goals-oriented training from top experts. You can rely on this innovative online tool to improve instruction in every classroom.

- Get unlimited, on-demand access to guided video and book content from top Solution Tree authors.

- Improve practices with personalized virtual coaching from PLC-certified trainers.

- Customize learning based on skill level and time commitments.